His
Intimate
Presence

Experiencing the Transforming Power
of the Holy Spirit

Bill Bright

His Intimate Presence

Published by
Campus Crusade for Christ
375 Hwy 74 South, Suite A
Peachtree City, GA 30265
www.campuscrusade.org

Design and production by Genesis Group

Cover by Operatunatea Publishing, Newnan, GA

Printed in the United States of America

ISBN 1-56399-192-6

Unless otherwise indicated, Scripture quotations are from the *New Living Translation*, © 1996 by Tyndale House Charitable Trust.

Scripture quotations designated NASB are from *The New American Standard Bible*, © 1960, 1962, 1963, 1968, 1971, 1972, 1973, 1975, 1977 by the Lockman Foundation, La Habra, California.

Scripture quotations designated TLB are from *The Living Bible*, © 1971 by Tyndale House Publishers, Wheaton, Illinois.

Scripture quotations designated NKJ are from the *New King James* version, © 1979, 1980, 1982 by Thomas Nelson Inc., Publishers, Nashville, Tennessee.

For more information, write:

Campus Crusade for Christ International—100 Lake Hart Drive, Orlando, FL 32832, USA

L.I.F.E., Campus Crusade for Christ—P.O. Box 40, Flemington Markets, 2129, Australia.

Campus Crusade for Christ of Canada—Box 529, Sumas, WA 98295

Campus Crusade for Christ—Fairgate House, King's Road, Tyseley, Birmingham, B11 2AA, United Kingdom

Lay Institute for Evangelism, Campus Crusade for Christ—P.O. Box 8786, Auckland, 1035, New Zealand

Campus Crusade for Christ—9 Lock Road #3-03, PacCan Centre, Singapore

Great Commission Movement of Nigeria—P.O. Box 500, Jos, Plateau State, Nigeria, West Africa

Special Thanks
to
Ted and Geneva Servais

They have greatly inspired and encouraged me
through their prayers and financial support of
this book and video project. I am deeply grateful.

Global Founding Partners

The Bright Media Foundation continues the multi-faceted ministries of Bill and Vonette Bright for generations yet unborn. God has touched and inspired them through the ministries of writers through the centuries. Likewise, they wish to pass along God's message in Jesus Christ as they have experienced it, seeking to inspire, train, and transform lives, thereby helping to fulfill the Great Commission each year until our Lord returns.

Many generous friends have prayed and sacrificed to support the Bright Media Foundation's culturally relevant, creative works, in print and electronic forms. The following persons specifically have helped to establish the Foundation. These special friends will always be known as *Global Founding Partners* of the Bright Media Foundation.

Bill and Christie Heavener and family
Stuart and Debra Sue Irby and family

To
Dr. Steve Douglass,
my successor as president of
Campus Crusade for Christ International

Since receiving Christ as my great God and Savior
in 1945, I have met many thousands of leaders
worldwide who were godly followers—servant
leaders of our Lord Jesus Christ. I cannot think of
anyone whose life and ministry demonstrates the
truths of this book more than Steve Douglass.
He is truly a Christian world statesman.

Contents

Acknowledgments

No project of this magnitude is ever completed without the wonderful assistance of many people committed to excellence and the truth of God's Word. I am grateful for each person who has helped me with this book.

The person and ministry of the Holy Spirit has been at the heart of my life and ministry for over fifty years. On hundreds of occasions I have written and spoken of His revolutionary person and power. But with the writing of *His Intimate Presence* I want to especially thank Nancy Schraeder and Cindy Godwin who have helped me put into this book the essence of what I have taught and sought to live for almost six decades. I am very grateful to them. I am also grateful to Robb Suggs for his wordsmithing and very appreciative of Helmut Teichert for his oversight of this project. I also want to thank the other team members for their significant contributions: Tammy Campbell and Lynn Copeland, editors; John Nill, publisher; and Michelle Treiber, cover coordinator and print broker.

There is one person more than any other who deserves special recognition: my beloved bride of over fifty years, Vonette. Together we have experienced the Holy Spirit's intimate presence in ministry and life day after day and year after year.

Introduction

There is a special person in my life, my very best friend, whom I would like for you to know as I do. He makes me glad. He fills my heart with joy. He inspires me with marvelous ideas. He energizes me. He surprises and blesses me daily. He listens when I need help. He has incredible wisdom and insight. When He speaks, it is as if a light goes on in my head and heart. He is my silent partner, and as a result I want everything I do to meet His approval. In fact, as I have gotten to know and have fellowship with Him since I met Him in 1945, I have come to the conviction that I do not want to do any-thing unless it is *His* idea. He is so tenderhearted, gracious, merciful, and kind that I never want to do anything that would displease or even disappoint Him.

Even when I feel a bit distant from Him, I have a great sense that He is still with me, that He will never leave me or turn His back on me. I can take to Him every challenge of my life—personal, professional, magnificent dreams and small worries, my joys, my unpleasantries, all of life's praise, all of life's problems—I share them with Him.

Now I want to share Him with you.

Just His presence is enough to keep me inspired and motivated. I am naturally shy and reserved; so many times in my life, if it were not for Him, I would have run away from opportunities, from meetings, and from trips. But because of Him, I have had the confidence to press ahead and see unbelievable, miraculous events unfold right before my eyes.

He was there when America saw the largest gathering of Christians in history for a training conference. More than 85,000 people per day for a week filled the Cotton Bowl in Dallas, Texas. He was there when I spoke to three million people at one time in Seoul, Korea. I watched through tears mixed with the rain as one million people stood to express assurance of their salvation through faith in Jesus Christ. He

11

was there in the precious moments when Vonette and I celebrated the arrival of our two sons, Zac and Brad. He was there when we decided that He should be not only our partner, but also the mastermind and general manager of everything we had or ever would have and everything we would ever do. He was with me in 1945 when He gave me a vision to produce a film on the life of Jesus. Since 1980, that film has been viewed by more than 5.25 billion persons in more than 850 languages. He was with me when I received the prestigious Templeton Prize of one million dollars for worldwide influence in religion. Recently, He has been with me in a series of hospitalizations and medical developments as I learned I have a terminal illness. I want you to know Him as I know Him because He has never failed me, whenever or whatever my need. He is not merely a help to me in surviving life's troubles; He gives me supernatural power to transcend these difficulties and keep me joyful on the journey.

I say with King David of Israel: "Taste and see that the Lord is good. Oh, the joys of those who trust in Him!" (Psalm 34:8). "Happy are those who hear the joyful call to worship, for they will walk in the light of Your presence, Lord. They rejoice all day long in Your wonderful reputation. They exult in Your righteousness" (Psalm 89:15,16).

I truly believe this book will help you come to know my friend, the Holy Spirit, the Spirit of our Lord Jesus Christ, in a personal, intimate way as never before. This knowledge is the greatest gift I can share with you. Determine now to spend time with Him, to get to know Him. Then give Him your life. With His help, we can give ourselves to helping fulfill the Great Commission each year until He returns to receive us unto Himself.

You and I will explore the amazing presence and power of God through the Holy Spirit, the Spirit of Jesus. We will uncover the marvelous, supernatural results of drawing close to God and inviting His Holy Spirit, the living Christ, to live in and through us. To present these exciting truths, I have chosen to divide this book into several sections.

In Part One, "A Divine Presence," we will explore the essential facts about the Holy Spirit and discover how each believer can be absolutely certain he or she is filled with the Spirit of God.

In Part Two, "An Intimate Presence," we will discover a number of exciting ministries the Spirit will perform in your life. We will learn the details of how the Holy Spirit acts as our teacher of God's truth, our helper in prayer, our motivator to holiness, our comforter in adversity, our peacemaker in the midst of conflict, our protector against the forces of evil, our source for service, our power for witnessing, and our counselor for decision-making.

In Part Three, "A Transforming Presence," I believe you will become excited as we paint a picture of your life in the transforming power of the Holy Spirit. We will uncover the abundant fruit of a Spirit-filled life, and discover how He brings spiritual revival into our lives.

As you prayerfully make your journey through this book, I believe God will begin to change you on the inside. It matters not where you are on your spiritual journey. You may be an experienced and active servant of God, or you may be a new believer. You may never have given the Holy Spirit much thought, or you may know more about Him than a seminary scholar. Whatever your situation may be, the truth of God's great love for us is irresistible. As you learn about each of the wonderful ministries of the Holy Spirit, I know you will be eager to surrender greater control of your life to the Holy Spirit who came to glorify Christ and lead us into all truth. You will want more of His comfort, more of His guidance and teaching, more of His power in ministry, and more of His fruit in evangelism.

I assure you that God wants you to have all these blessings and more. The Bible tells us that He has been waiting since the foundation of the universe to unfold the wonderful plans He has for you, and through the power of the Holy Spirit you can know and embrace those plans. I pray that God will use this very book to draw you closer to Himself, to fill you with His Spirit, and to send you on a ministry that will influence the world for Christ.

I pray too that God's richest blessings and power will enhance your enjoyment of the wonderful presence and power of the Holy Spirit every moment for the rest of your life.

Part One

A Divine
Presence

Chapter 1

Where Is God When I Need Him?

As the crowded elevator approached the first-floor lobby, Katie had never felt more alone. Her entire world had come unraveled in one catastrophic moment.

She had just left the doctor's office with a diagnosis of pancreatic cancer. How could she have been prepared for such a blow? She had children to care for, a husband to love, and a crowded agenda of activities. After a decade of marriage, Katie and Brad were looking forward to the next one, and several more after that. They were anticipating doing more traveling. They were planning to savor the pleasure of growing old together and spoiling their grandchildren. Cancer was nowhere in the itinerary. Where was God? How could He let the unthinkable destroy her future?

Katie was not the only miserable person on that elevator. With trembling fingers, Justin was clutching a box with his personal possessions. He had just cleaned out his desk after being given a pink slip. Sure, everyone hits an occasional bump in the professional road. But for Justin, the timing could not have been worse. He had just made a down payment on a new house. Friends had told him to stretch financially when investing in a home, and he had taken their advice. The plan was to work some overtime and climb the corporate ladder. He had never imagined he would be fired. And he still had his college loan to pay off. Suddenly he was left with no income and a world of debt. Justin thought he did not have a prayer of finding another job quickly. Speaking of prayer, what about God? Was He even listening?

17

Standing next to Justin was Carl, deep in tortuous thought. The night before, his wife had walked into the room and found him viewing pornography on the Internet. Disgusted and disappointed, she rushed from the room. The silence in the house had been suffocating. Carl was a good father and a successful businessman, and he went to church. But the stranglehold pornography had on him when he was single did not go away when he married. He struggled with pornography throughout his marriage. When his wife had discovered the magazines and videos, he had promised, repeatedly, that he would never buy them again. But now pornography was all around him, just the press of a button away. Why was it so easy to fall into sin?

Yet another person stood in this elevator, a young woman named Becky. She and her boyfriend, David, had been dating for over two years. Two days ago, he told her he wanted out. She was devastated. They had shopped for engagement rings and talked about wedding plans. Because they were going to be married, she thought it was okay that they had gone further sexually than she intended. Having David as a boyfriend had given her such a sense of purpose and value. Now, instead of feeling important and loved, she felt empty and abandoned. Where was God and the fulfillment He had promised?

Perhaps you've felt like Justin or Katie, or like Carl or Becky or someone else on that elevator full of ordinary folks heading down to life's depths. We all reach crisis points when we can do nothing but cry out to God in pain and confusion. We have all had black moments when we have suspected, in the darkest part of our souls, that maybe He simply is not listening. Maybe He does not even care.

Just when we find ourselves moving along under the illusion that we are self-sufficient, handling life well, and standing on our own two feet, life has a way of reminding us that we are but small, helpless children. We discover there are forces too great for us to overcome alone. So we run crying to the Lord as little children, seeking comfort and answers.

But how does God feel about that? Is He cold and indifferent, reminding us that everybody else has problems, too? Or does He take us into His arms with love and compassion?

God Longs for You to Know Him Intimately

There is nothing cold or indifferent about the God I have known for nearly six decades. The Bible says that He is love and that He never stops desiring an ever-closer relationship with us. My experience has shown that to be true.

God has a wonderful plan for every single one of us, no matter what our circumstances may be. The greatest part of that plan is for us to know Him intimately—to enjoy the deepest and most fulfilling relationship we can possibly have. He expressed this desire in a profound way. The most profound depth of love is sacrifice, and our Lord has made the greatest sacrifice possible out of His love for us. He put aside His power, rights, and splendor as Creator of the universe in order to rescue us from the consequences of our own sin. As a tiny, helpless baby He came to the world He had created, in a universe He ruled, and He made Himself known to us as Jesus of Nazareth.

Fully God and fully human, Jesus lived among us and demonstrated through His life and teachings just how we are supposed to live. He was the Word of God made flesh. Then, on the cross where men crucified Him, He paid the penalty for our sins. He took on our punishment so that we might be spared to enjoy eternal life and an intimate relationship with Him. He rose from the dead as the "first fruit" of this new order, just as we, too, will rise again.

Then something incredible and marvelous happened. When Jesus returned to heaven to sit at the right hand of the Father, He made a way to remain among us as long as we live on this earth. He released His Holy Spirit to come and live inside each one of His followers. In that way, we have the mind and the Spirit of Jesus living within us.

That is why He told His disciples that it was better for them that He leave this world (John 16:6,7). They had only enjoyed the presence of Jesus among them physically. Now and for all time, He is among us in the deepest and most powerful way, living within our hearts. We have Jesus' counsel, comfort, strength, and friendship with us wherever we go, and nothing we or anyone can do will ever take it away. The Bible tells us this is a preview, a foretaste, of the wonderful fellowship that lies ahead of us when we join Him in eternity.

Many years ago I was struck with the reality of this truth. Why is it that God is with us and within us, yet so many of us live our lives with little awareness of His presence? We face life's problems without taking advantage of His wisdom. We cope with crises without calling upon the limitless strength that He has to offer us. Have you made that mistake in your own life? Why does this happen?

It certainly is not because God wants it to be so. Psalm 145:18 tells us, "The LORD is close to all who call on Him, yes, to all who call on Him sincerely." That means the Lord longs to maintain an intimate relationship with every one of us. I believe the key word in that verse is *sincerely*. How sincere are you in calling upon the Lord? Do you really want to have a daily dependence upon Him? Or are you simply looking for instant help from the immediate problem of the day? Do you wish to partake in a rich and full relationship with the King of all kings? Or are you concerned that He might interfere with the way you want to run your life?

Those impure motives will never cause God to stop reaching out to you, but they will make it much more difficult for you to know the fullness of His love and power. Only when we finally come to a sincere desire for Him, as the psalm indicates, will we discover what He has wanted us to have all along.

The Spirit of Christ in You

The Lord desires daily fellowship with us through the Holy Spirit, whom He sent to indwell each of us. The moment you accept God's gift of salvation and receive Christ into your life, He enters your heart in the person of the Holy Spirit. Though you may not always be aware of Him, He takes permanent residence inside you. If you are a Christian, the Spirit of Christ remains within you every moment of every day.

Have you ever stopped to count the many ways the Holy Spirit ministers to your life? I find my heart filled with deep gratitude and my emotions stirred within me when I enumerate them. The Spirit transforms our lives through a new birth. He provides comfort to us in difficult times. He strengthens us when we are weak. He intercedes for us even when we do not know how to pray. He teaches us God's truth. He bears witness with our spirit that we belong to God. He sets us apart for holy service to the Lord. He refreshes us deep in our souls. He produces the fruit of the Spirit in our lives. He unifies all believers everywhere. He enables us to lead holy lives that are pleasing to God. He brings us the ultimate joy and gives us a deep, inner peace which nothing can disturb. Above all, He empowers us to complete the mission Jesus Christ came to accomplish—to seek and save the lost (Luke 19:10).

The most wonderful thing about this plan is the way Jesus multiplied His ministry to all of us. When He walked among us physically, His time was limited. He could only be in one place at one time, and with only a few people. Living as a man limited His physical reach. But as He lives within us in the person of the Holy Spirit, there are no limits on our access to Him. Any time, any place, every believer can live in the wonderful presence of God. And we have the same Friend and Comforter whom the first Christians had some two thousand years ago.

If you are a Christian, the Spirit of Christ remains within you every moment of every day.

You and I have either never heard or have forgotten what is available to us through the Holy Spirit. We think, "If only I could talk to Jesus as the disciples were able to do! If only I could sit at His feet, hear His teachings, and see His miracles. Life would be so much simpler and so much less frightening if I had God in the flesh right here beside me." Yes, it would be wonderful to look into the eyes of Jesus and ask Him the deepest questions of our lives. But have you ever studied the disciples' lives before and after the Holy Spirit came to them? I believe it is very important to explore how the Holy Spirit made a difference in them.

The Impact of the Holy Spirit

It is easy for us to envy the disciples. After all, they had physical access to Jesus for three full years. They accompanied Him on His travels, heard every word of His teachings, and saw His incredible miracles. They were able to ask Him questions, and the Bible shows us they took advantage of that opportunity. Finally, after He ascended to heaven to sit at the right hand of the Father, Jesus' disciples received the Holy Spirit, whom Jesus sent, as recorded in Acts chapter 2.

The four Gospels present the disciples as being rather childish and inept when Jesus was among them physically. They were often slow to understand the concepts He was teaching. They held many of the same misconceptions and prejudices as the general population of that time. They had rivalries and quarrels that are almost embarrassing for us to read about today. Anyone might have wondered how these disciples could ever be capable of carrying on the ministry that Jesus began.

Our Lord constantly corrected them as they experienced failures of faith, misunderstandings of His purpose, and the inability to grasp what lay ahead in Jerusalem—even though He told them clearly that the time was coming for Him to be executed. When He led His inner circle of disciples to pray with Him in the garden on that fateful night, they kept falling asleep. Then, when He was arrested, their courage failed. All except John fled in terror and fear, despite all the wonderful things they had seen Him do. After His crucifixion, they made no attempt even to claim the body or help with funeral arrangements.

These were His best and closest friends, and His arrest left them frightened, discouraged, defeated, and fruitless. If the story had ended there, it's likely no Gospels would ever have been written—and Jesus would be an obscure footnote in Palestinian history. Praise God that the greatest story ever told did not end there! When Jesus left them for the final time, He sent the Holy Spirit. And history is quite clear about the quality of the disciples' lives after that event.

Upon Jesus' arrest, Peter had denied his relationship with his Master three times before a small crowd. But Acts 2 tells us that after the Spirit came, this same Peter preached a public sermon so powerful that three thousand people received Jesus as their Lord and Savior (Acts 2:1–41). What an incredible upgrade in courage in so short a time!

Peter and the other disciples continued to preach, often in the face of Roman hostility. When Peter and John were arrested and brought before the authorities, "the members of the council were amazed when they saw the boldness of Peter and John, for they could see that they were ordinary men who had had no special training" (Acts 4:13). Actually, they had received the most special training possible over a three-year period. What made the difference at this point was the presence of the Holy Spirit. These men seemed to be completely new men with no resemblance to the confused, childish, and fearful followers Jesus had led for three years.

They were indeed completely different, due to the transforming power of the Holy Spirit. Despite the intimidating power of the massive Roman Empire and the religious leaders, the disciples became men who changed the very history of the world. The Spirit of God brings the most amazing power that can possibly be released upon the world. It was true in the days of the early Church and it is still true today. God wants you to walk in the same power and victory as those world-shaking disciples of two thousand years ago.

The Gentle Whisper of the Holy Spirit

At this point you might well ask, "Why don't I experience God dramatically, as those early believers did? Why do I not see anyone experiencing God that way?" A man from Old Testament times, a prophet named Elijah, struggled with the same issue in 1 Kings 19.

Elijah lived in a day, much like today, when many people doubted or scoffed at God. He longed to see God move with tremendous power and silence the critics. Sometimes God did that. But there was also a time when Elijah's very life was in danger, and God seemed silent. An evil and godless queen named Jezebel sent her armies on a mission to kill Elijah, and the prophet became angry and frustrated. Was this his reward for being loyal and faithful to God? Why didn't the Lord stretch out His arm to defend an obedient servant? Elijah's depression and despair cut so deep that, resting beneath a tree, he finally asked God to simply let him die. If God wasn't going to speak or act, and if seemingly no one but Elijah served the true Lord anyway, what was the point of living?

God taught Elijah an unforgettable lesson. He sent the ailing prophet to a mountain and commanded him to stand and watch as the Lord passed. Wasn't that what Elijah wanted, after all? His heart must have raced as he anticipated looking upon the manifest glory of God with his own two eyes.

> As Elijah stood there, the LORD passed by, and a mighty windstorm hit the mountain. It was such a terrible blast that the rocks were torn loose, but the LORD was not in the wind. After the wind there was an earthquake, but the LORD was not in the earthquake. And after the earthquake there was a fire, but the LORD was not in the fire. And after the fire there was the sound of a gentle whisper (1 Kings 19:11,12).

Elijah understood the message God was sending him. God can hurl windstorms whenever He chooses. He can make the earth tremble or set it aflame. He has the power to do these and more. But He usually does not choose to move among us in spectacular or sensational ways, but rather in the sound of a gentle whisper.

Elijah had seen God move differently on an earlier mountaintop. At Mount Carmel, God had sent fire from heaven in the judgment of false prophets from the Baal religion (1 Kings 18). But most of the time, as has been my experience, the voice of God is soft and subtle. Please do not miss His voice by assuming it must be loud and dramatic. We often come to God with very direct questions: "Is this the person I should marry?" Or, "Is that the life vocation You desire for me?" How convenient it would be for us if God would simply write His answer in the clouds. We long to hear an audible voice, or see a stroke of lightning that etches His directions upon a tree.

But God is not interested in simple convenience. He wants us to know Him as our Friend and Lord. He desires that we know Him well enough to learn to hear His still, small voice, even when it is as gentle as a whisper. True friendship is never quick or convenient. We must work at it over a long period.

Perhaps God's answer to you will become evident in a deep study of His Word. Perhaps you will hear it in the wise counsel of a friend. Perhaps it will emerge through long, searching times of prayer and fellowship with Him. He wants us to know Him well and to love Him deeply. The Holy Spirit helps us do that. For many years I have lived according to the verse, "It is God who works in you to will and to act according to His good purpose" (Philippians 2:13, NIV).

Where is God when you need Him? He is with you, beside you, within you. Let us learn to listen for a lifetime. Then we can sing in praise, with David the psalmist:

I can never escape from Your spirit!
I can never get away from Your presence!
If I go up to heaven, You are there;
if I go down to the place of the dead, You are there.
If I ride the wings of the morning,
if I dwell by the farthest oceans,
even there Your hand will guide me,
and Your strength will support me.
(Psalm 139:7–10)

Life Application

 Meditate on the Words of the Spirit. God has revealed Himself to us through the Bible. The Holy Spirit spoke gently to the writers of each book, and He speaks to us through them. We can develop a deeper relationship with our Creator by reading and meditating upon these words. Memorize the following verses:

- "The LORD is close to all who call on Him, yes, to all who call on Him sincerely" (Psalm 145:18).

- "The LORD is close to the brokenhearted; He rescues those who are crushed in spirit" (Psalm 34:18).

 Focus on the Presence of the Spirit. Prayerfully answer these questions:

- How would you honestly describe your picture of God?

- How would you depict your relationship with God?

- How have you sensed God's presence in your life?

- Has God ever seemed distant to you during times of crisis?

- How are you pursuing the intimate relationship that God desires with you?

 Walk in the Power of the Spirit. Let the following prayer lead you in a time of honest reflection before God:

Dear heavenly Father, I know that You made me and You love me. I thank You that because of Christ's death on the cross for my sins, I can come to You as Your child. I ask you to forgive me of my sins and my wrong perceptions of You. Please renew my love for You and help me trust You completely. Thank You that You have sent Your Holy Spirit to live within me. You commanded me to be filled with the Holy Spirit and You promised that You will hear and answer any prayer that is in harmony with Your will. So by faith, I invite You to fill me with Your Holy Spirit. In Your Son's marvelous name—Jesus! Amen.

Chapter 2

Who Is the Holy Spirit?

David Livingstone was the first Western man to explore much of central Africa one hundred and fifty years ago. He had a passion for that beautiful continent where the gospel had yet to be taken. He led expeditions that pushed deeper and deeper into the jungles and savannahs—often thousands of miles at a stretch.

In November 1855, while traveling along the Zambezi River in south-central Africa, Livingstone became the first European to set eyes on Victoria Falls. Those who have seen this natural wonder understand how incredible a sight it is. The massive falls plunge 360 feet to the earth below. Some in Livingstone's party might have thought they had discovered the world's greatest untapped source of natural power. But as Livingstone knew, they had done no such thing. There is a source infinitely more powerful.

When you discover what it means for the Holy Spirit to be active in your life, you experience a power greater than anything on earth. The power from a hydroelectric dam can light up a city, providing hundreds of thousands of people with electricity. But the power of the Holy Spirit touches eternity itself. Unfortunately, to most people this power is just as hidden and mysterious as Victoria Falls was in the days before Livingstone. The modern world's ignorance of the Holy Spirit is far more pervasive than most of us realize.

A well-known church in California recently commissioned Christian pollster George Barna to conduct a survey of their congregation. Some of the findings astonished the researchers. The church discovered that over half of the congregation did not believe that the Holy Spirit was a living entity![1] And this is a solid, Bible-believing church.

Much of the mystery and ignorance comes, of course, through the fact that God's Spirit transcends our five senses of sight, hearing, taste, touch, and smell. He can be perceived only by our spirit—that unseen part of us that is renewed at salvation. Through our spirit we now have a relationship with the living God, who is Spirit. We cannot touch Him physically, though we can be touched emotionally by Him. We cannot see Him, yet He refines our vision and understanding of our awesome Creator and Savior. We cannot hear His voice, but we can listen for His guidance.

God's Spirit can be perceived only by our spirit—that unseen part of us that is renewed at salvation.

Although so many are ignorant of the truth about the Holy Spirit, that truth can be found in the Bible. In the Old Testament He is mentioned 80 times and referred to by fifteen different names. Among them are the Spirit of God (Genesis 1:2), Spirit of the LORD (Judges 11:29), Holy Spirit (Psalm 51:11), and My Spirit (Joel 2:28).

In the New Testament, 271 references are made to the Holy Spirit. He is called by nine different names: the Holy Spirit (Matthew 1:18), Spirit of God (Matthew 3:16), My Spirit (Matthew 12:18), Spirit of Truth (John 15:26), Counselor (John 14:26), Spirit of the Lord (Acts 5:9), Spirit of Christ (1 Peter 1:11), Spirit of your Father (Matthew 10:20), and Spirit of Jesus (Acts 16:7).

There are many names for the Holy Spirit, but also many misconceptions about Him. Perhaps this is because He is impossible to picture in our minds. With some effort, most of us can form mental images of God the Father and God the Son. We can read about God and His dealings with His people in the Old Testament. We can read about Jesus in the New Testament. We can understand their relationship by watching how earthly fathers and sons relate to each other. It is considerably more difficult to understand the Holy Spirit.

We cannot visualize Him. We have no earthly model to help us comprehend Him and His work, and He never speaks of Himself—His role is to glorify the Father and the Son. So how do we grasp the identity of the Holy Spirit? Let us examine three essential truths.

The Holy Spirit Is a Person

Many people make the mistake of depersonalizing God's Holy Spirit. They think of Him as some kind of will or force within them, not a *He* but an *It*. They confuse Him with the vague generic idea of a conscience, or pick up false ideas from Eastern religions about some small "spark" of God within mankind. But the Bible is very clear that none of these accurately describe who the Holy Spirit is and how He relates to us.

God's Spirit is fully a person with all His own individual traits. He speaks, inspires, guides, convicts, comforts, and encourages—all functions an individual personality might perform. Jesus always referred to Him in that light. He used the personal pronouns *He* and *Him*, but never the impersonal pronoun *It*. When He spoke to His disciples in the upper room about the Holy Spirit, He used the Greek word *paracletos* meaning "called to one's side." That name tells us that the Holy Spirit has the ability to give aid and to comfort or console.[2]

As a true personality and not a nebulous "force," the Spirit has a number of personal traits, as illustrated by the following verses.

- **The Holy Spirit has knowledge**: "We know these things because God has revealed them to us by His Spirit, and His Spirit searches out everything and shows us even God's deep secrets. No one can know what anyone else is really thinking except that person alone, and no one can know God's thoughts except God's own Spirit" (1 Corinthians 2:10,11).

- **The Holy Spirit can be grieved**: "Do not bring sorrow to God's Holy Spirit by the way you live. Remember, He is the one who has identified you as His own, guaranteeing that you will be saved on the day of redemption" (Ephesians 4:30).

- **The Holy Spirit has a will:** "It is the one and only Holy Spirit who distributes these gifts. He alone decides which gift each person should have" (1 Corinthians 12:11).

- **The Holy Spirit expresses love:** "I urge you, brothers, by our Lord Jesus Christ and by the love of the Spirit, to join me in my struggle by praying to God for me" (Romans 15:30, NIV).

- **The Holy Spirit can be lied to:** "Then Peter said, 'Ananias, why has Satan filled your heart? You lied to the Holy Spirit, and you kept some of the money for yourself...You weren't lying to us but to God'" (Acts 5:3,4).

- **The Holy Spirit speaks to us:** "One day as these men were worshiping the Lord and fasting, the Holy Spirit said, 'Dedicate Barnabas and Saul for the special work I have for them'" (Acts 13:2).

- **The Holy Spirit teaches us:** "When the Father sends the Counselor as My representative—and by the Counselor I mean the Holy Spirit—he will teach you everything and will remind you of everything I Myself have told you" (John 14:26).

- **The Holy Spirit guides us:** "When the Spirit of truth comes, He will guide you into all truth" (John 16:13).

God's Spirit is not only a Person, but a Person with a vibrant and powerful personality. He is a unique member of the Trinity. As you learn more about His work in your life, you will be more aware of His presence and power. You will recognize His gentle voice, welcoming His comfort and basking in His encouragement. He will come to be like a perfect Friend, who will be with you everywhere you go.

The Holy Spirit Is God

As we have explored these truths about the Spirit as part of the Trinity, I anticipate that a few questions have formed in your mind. These are questions that people have had in every age—questions about the relationship among God the Father, God the Son (Jesus Christ), and God the Holy Spirit. Let us examine these issues with care.

The Bible proclaims that God is one yet triune. That is, He exists as three Persons in one. How can God be one and three at the same time?

The Bible has many references to the fact that God is triune. At creation, God declared, "Let Us make people in Our image, to be like Ourselves" (Genesis 1:26). After mankind fell into sin, the LORD God said, "The people have become as We are, knowing everything, both good and evil" (Genesis 3:22).

Romans 1:4 says, "Jesus Christ our Lord was shown to be the Son of God when God powerfully raised Him from the dead by means of the Holy Spirit."

All the while, the Bible states that God is one: "Hear, O Israel: The LORD our God, the LORD is one" (Deuteronomy 6:4, NIV).

Centuries ago, one of the world's most gifted thinkers and theologians, Saint Augustine, pondered the concept of the Trinity as he strolled along the beach. He noticed a boy running back and forth with a bucket attempting to fill a small hole in the sand with water. When Augustine asked the boy what he was doing, he replied, "I am trying to put the ocean into this hole." Augustine understood that he was even then attempting something equally impossible. He was trying to "put an infinite God into his finite mind."[3] Our finite minds are simply not capable of completely understanding the divine nature of God who created 100 to 200 billion galaxies.

It can be argued that water is the most important substance on earth. All living things need it to survive. Water is defined chemically as H_2O, a molecule made up of hydrogen and oxygen. It can exist in three states—liquid, ice, and steam. But it is always the same substance—H_2O. This fact of God's creation is a limited and imperfect illustration, but it helps us get on the right track in considering the mystery of the Trinity. However, when we come to believe we have the mystery solved, we are fooling ourselves! As finite human beings, we will never comprehend the depths of the mystery.

I do not understand how God can be one and three, but there are many mysteries I embrace despite my inability to master them. I accept, by faith, what the Bible tells me about God. God, who has revealed Himself to us in three Persons, is one, and the Holy Spirit is the third Person of that Trinity.

Before Jesus ascended into heaven, He commanded His followers to "go and make disciples of all the nations, baptizing them in the name of the Father and the Son and *the Holy Spirit*" (Matthew 28:19, emphasis added). Jesus knew that His disciples could not complete on their own what God wanted them to do. That is why He sent the Holy Spirit, who is the Spirit of Christ, to live within all believers (Romans 8:9).

The Holy Spirit is co-equal with God the Father and God the Son (John 14:16). He possesses all the attributes of God: He is all-powerful, all-knowing, ever-present, sovereign, holy, absolute truth, righteous, just, loving, merciful, faithful, and never-changing. He is not a servant of God or a lesser expression of the Lord. He is in every sense the living God.

The Holy Spirit Has a Mission

The Holy Spirit has been at work in the world since creation, and He temporarily indwelt certain individuals in the Old Testament for specific purposes (for example, see Exodus 31:2,3; 1 Samuel 16:13,14; Ezekiel 2:2). When He came at Pentecost, however, it was to permanently indwell all believers and to accomplish a network of missions and ministries.

First, *the Holy Spirit came to convict the world of sin and lead us into all truth*. It is through the Holy Spirit's work in our lives that we come to recognize our sin and our need for a Savior. He then draws us to God's truth and to the salvation that is available only through Jesus Christ. Did you know that you can never come to salvation unless the Holy Spirit is involved? Jesus said, "The truth is, no one can enter the Kingdom of God without being born of water and the Spirit" (John 3:5). When you share your faith with a nonbeliever, it is the Spirit who is at work, convicting the person of his sin and drawing him to God.

Second, *God sent His Holy Spirit to glorify Christ*. Jesus proclaimed regarding the Holy Spirit, "He will bring Me glory by revealing to you whatever He receives from Me" (John 16:14). The Spirit glorifies the Lord by always bringing honor to the name of Jesus. This is one of the primary ways we recognize the Spirit in someone's life: If Jesus is exalted and held high, this is a sign that the Holy Spirit is at work. Believers who are controlled by the Spirit will not take the credit for the good things they accomplish in His power; the glory is always directed toward Jesus Christ.

Third, *the Holy Spirit's mission is to empower believers.* Just before Jesus was crucified, He made the most startling promise of His entire ministry to His disciples. He proclaimed, "The truth is, anyone who believes in Me will do the same works I have done, and even greater works, because I am going to be with the Father. You can ask for anything in My name, and I will do it" (John 14:12,13). The disciples must have been stunned! Jesus fed thousands and enabled the blind to see. I was amazed the first time I read that promise, and I am still in awe fifty-five years later. The truth is that we have no power within ourselves to serve God; supernatural power is needed, and the Spirit provides it.

As we have seen, the disciples were powerless even with the constant presence of Jesus among them. But after the Holy Spirit came at Pentecost, they boldly proclaimed the good news of Jesus' resurrection. The entrance of the Spirit into the lives of the first Christians was like turning on a power transformer.

It is through the Spirit's work in our lives that we come to recognize our sin and our need for a Savior.

The Holy Spirit can transform you in the same way. The promise Jesus made, that His followers would exceed His achievements, applies as much to you as to Peter, James, or John. Have you longed to live a fruitful life for your Lord? Have you been frustrated and fearful about sharing your faith? You need not and must not lean on your own power, for that strategy is bound to fail. You cannot do a wonderful thing for God by yourself any more than you can equal the power of Victoria Falls with your kitchen faucet!

The great evangelist D. L. Moody learned this truth through his own experience. He had a good heart, and he was trying to do all that he could to glorify God. But there was something missing from his preaching, his planning, and every area in which he tried to serve the Lord. A group of women saw his unhappiness and understood exactly what was missing from his ministry. They began to meet daily and pray that the presence of the Holy Spirit would overwhelm Moody in his work, and give him the power he was missing. One day Moody was walking down a street in New York City when suddenly, without any warning, a sense of the power and goodness of God came over him. The Lord revealed Himself to Moody right there on the street, and the evangelist was totally overcome. From that moment on, his ministry was completely transformed. He often told his friends that he was preaching the same sermons; he was following the same strategies. But the Spirit of God had gotten involved in his ministry, and now unlimited power flowed through everything he did.

In all my decades of ministry, I have seen the Spirit transform believers and their work time after time. The Spirit has led Campus Crusade to use many different strategies and to found many new ministries. Our leaders will not take one single step unless we are fully persuaded that the Spirit of God is involved and is leading us in that direction. Otherwise our efforts will be doomed to failure, and we will be miserable and frustrated indeed.

What about your life and work? Is the Holy Spirit filling you daily and equipping you for service, or do you feel the frustration of trying to live the supernatural life by natural means? God wants a life of excitement and fulfillment for you. Jesus came, and then sent His Spirit, so that you could experience an abundant life. That life is available only when you experience the enabling of the Holy Spirit as a way of life. He will draw you every day to know Him in a deeper, more intimate way.

Do you desire to overcome past failures and destructive habits and experience a victorious life? Do you long for your marriage, your relationships, and your work to move beyond the commonplace and reflect the amazing love and integrity of Christ? Do you wish for your life to further God's marvelous eternal plan? Then you must surrender yourself to God's presence within you—His Holy Spirit!

In the next chapter we will explore how the Holy Spirit can make a supernatural difference in your life.

Life Application

 Meditate on the Words of the Spirit. Memorize and meditate on the following verses from this chapter:

- "I will ask the Father, and He will give you another Counselor to be with you forever—the Spirit of truth" (John 14:16, 17, NIV).

- "We know these things because God has revealed them to us by His Spirit, and His Spirit searches out everything and shows us even God's deep secrets" (1 Corinthians 2:10).

 Focus on the Presence of the Spirit. Contemplate the following questions:

- How would you describe the Holy Spirit?

- How has the Holy Spirit made you aware of His presence in your life?

- What are some areas in your life that could greatly benefit from the control of the Holy Spirit? Make a list and surrender each area to God. Ask Him to cleanse you from all your sins and enable you by His Holy Spirit to live a victorious life.

 Walk in the Power of the Spirit. Make the following your own heartfelt prayer:

> Dear Lord, thank you for sending Your Holy Spirit to live in me. My life would be so dark without Your presence. Thank You that You are a personal God, and that I can know You intimately. Thank You that Your Holy Spirit loves, teaches, and speaks to me and lives Christ's life through me. Help me to be aware, moment by moment, of Your Holy Spirit working in my life and in the world around me. May my Lord and Savior Jesus Christ be more and more glorified through me. Amen.

Chapter 3

How Can I
Be Filled with
the Holy Spirit?

M any years ago, as D. L. Moody was preparing to lead a series
of meetings in England, an elderly pastor wanted to know,
"Why do we need this Mr. Moody? He is uneducated and
inexperienced. Who does he think he is anyway? Does he think he
has a monopoly on the Holy Spirit?"

A wise colleague smiled and responded, "No, but the Holy Spirit
has a monopoly on Mr. Moody."[1]

As a young man, Moody was discouraged from preaching because
he felt thoroughly unequipped as a communicator. But as we have
seen, Moody surrendered himself completely to the Holy Spirit and
was filled with His power. From that day forward, his life and ministry began to bear much fruit for the Lord. He said, "I believe firmly
that the moment our hearts are emptied of pride and selfishness and
ambition and everything that is contrary to God's law, the Holy Spirit
will fill every corner of our hearts. But if we are full of pride and con-
ceit and ambition and the world, there is no room for the Spirit of
God. We must be emptied before we can be filled."[2]

We want to be filled with the living water that never runs dry—but
first we have to confess our sins to the Lord so He can remove the
impurities from our lives. The all-powerful, loving Creator of the universe wishes to take full control of the smallest details of our lives.
There is no limit to what He might accomplish through us if we sim-

ply yield to His Lordship. Yet too often we fill our lives with unworthy things, and we leave no room for the Holy Spirit.

Apart from Him, nothing you attempt to do can have any ultimate worth; through His Spirit, *all* things are possible.

How to Know Whether You Are Filled by the Holy Spirit

Please rest assured that if you are a Christian, that is, if you have sincerely asked Jesus to come into your life as your Savior, Lord, and Master, then the Holy Spirit has already made a home in your heart. The moment you surrendered your life to Jesus, the Spirit came in—even if you did not feel anything. Our faith is based on fact rather than feelings. The *Four Spiritual Laws* booklet uses a train diagram to illustrate this. The train is pulled by *fact*, which is followed by the *faith* car. *Feeling* is the caboose. We are fact-driven, not feeling-driven believers.

After the Spirit comes into your life through the new birth, He remains in residence. Why, then, do so many believers see no evidence of that fact? Why do they feel powerless? The answer is that it is one thing to *host* the Holy Spirit. It is another to be *filled* with the Holy Spirit.

It has often been said that the Spirit can be *resident* without being *"president."* You can yield control to Him all of the time, some of the time, or none of the time. After salvation itself, this is perhaps the greatest concern of all. The choice is up to you. You have a free will to either obey God or disobey God.

How, then, can you know you are filled with the Holy Spirit? First, recognize that He is present, and He will never leave you. Second, look for the evidence of His work in your life. Here are a few questions you might ask yourself:

- Do you feel the joy and vitality of serving God?
- Do you desire to spend time with God through prayer and His inspired Word?
- Do your relationships increasingly honor and glorify Christ?

- Are you regularly, fruitfully sharing your faith in Christ with non-believers?

- Are you growing in faith and in the knowledge of God daily?

- Is God leading you out into regular, productive ministry?

- Is there evidence of the fruit of the Spirit in your life? (See Chapter 13.)

- Are you using your spiritual gifts to serve the body of Christ? (See Chapter 10.)

Obstacles to Being Filled with the Holy Spirit

It is sad to recognize the truth: our enemy, the devil, has any number of weapons to keep us from relying upon the Holy Spirit to strengthen and guide us in living for Christ. It is important to consider a few of these weapons.

Prideful Self-Reliance. Pride is the most basic of sins; it confronts each one of us. Our pride places our own self-will on the throne of our lives, rather than Christ. This "me-first" attitude, of course, is one to which the Scriptures are completely opposed.

The truth of Scripture reminds me that I am crucified, dead, buried, and raised to newness of life with Christ (Romans 6). My flesh, the old Bill Bright, is at war with God. It never did please God and never will (Romans 8:7).

In many words and ways, I daily acknowledge (according to these wonderful truths as well as Colossians 3 and other passages) that the old Bill Bright is dead and should have as little desire for this world as a dead man. I am alive to Christ, a suit of clothes for Him. I invite Him, in all of His resurrection love and power, to control my thoughts, desires, attitudes, actions, and words. As it says in Galatians 2:20, "I have been crucified with Christ and I no longer live, but Christ lives in me. The life I live in the body, I live by faith in the Son of God, who loved me and gave Himself for me" (NIV).

Worldliness. We often become so intrigued with the false treasures of this world that we lose sight of the blessings God has for us.

41

Jesus proclaimed to His followers, "How do you benefit if you gain the whole world but lose your own soul in the process?" (Mark 8:36). In 1 Corinthians 7:31 we are told that "this world and all it contains will pass away."

Many years ago, Vonette and I made a commitment in writing—a commitment that we would not fall prey to worldliness but instead sign over every present and future material, intellectual, and spiritual possession to Him. That covenant has been the very key to any success we have enjoyed in ministry and in helping to build God's kingdom.

The Approval of Others. Undue concern for popular opinion can stand in the way of all that God would like to do in your life. King Solomon, the wisest man who ever lived, wrote, "The fear of man brings a snare, but he who trusts in the LORD will be exalted" (Proverbs 29:25, NASB). Psalm 1 describes the trusting believer this way:

> Oh, the joys of those who do not follow evil men's advice, who do not hang around with sinners, scoffing at the things of God: but they delight in doing everything God wants them to, and day and night are always meditating on His laws and thinking about ways to follow Him more closely.
>
> They are like trees along a river bank bearing luscious fruit each season without fail. Their leaves shall never wither, and all they do shall prosper (Psalm 1:1–3, TLB).

Lack of Faith. Some believers cannot summon the will to place themselves completely in God's hands. How could it be that He has yet to earn our complete loving faith? The Bible tells us He knew us even before He formed us in the womb. He cherishes the plans He has for us, as any Father does for His child. Yet we withhold our dependence upon Him.

For over fifty years, my wife and I have taken God at His Word, and we can assure you that He is more than faithful. As I mentioned above, we as a couple signed away our lives to God in an act of faith, one Sunday afternoon over half a century ago. We have never looked back. We literally wrote out and signed a contract, committing ourselves to living as slaves of Jesus. This was the most significant event of our lives, apart from salvation. It has influenced every decision we have made for over fifty years. Approximately twenty-four hours after signing that contract, God gave me the vision for a worldwide movement to help fulfill the Great Commission, a movement called Campus Crusade for Christ. I sincerely believe that had we not signed that contract, God would not have given me that vision. No doubt, the hundreds of millions who have been drawn to Christ through the Campus Crusade ministry are the direct fruit of our faithful leap into our Father's arms, to trust Him completely. Thousands of our fellow staff later joined us in total surrender to Him.

The most important question in your life is whether you have truly trusted Christ not just as your Savior, but as your Lord, Master, and King.

Undue concern for popular opinion can stand in the way of all that God would like to do in your life.

Unconfessed Sin. Although Jesus has provided forgiveness for all sins—past, present, and future—we rob ourselves of intimacy with God through our disobedience. The prophet Isaiah offers us a perfect description of this regular event in the lives of all believers: "There is a problem—your sins have cut you off from God. Because of your sin, He has turned away and will not listen anymore" (Isaiah 59:2).

In order to stay in intimate fellowship with our loving Lord, we must confess any sin—in thought, word, or deed—as soon as we become aware of it. James 4:8 admonishes us, "Draw close to God, and God will draw close to you. Wash your hands, you sinners; purify your hearts, you hypocrites." To confess your sins is to experience His wonderful cleansing. Your relationship with our holy God will be restored to newness and greater intimacy.

I hope you make a habit of immediately confessing your sins as they occur. The most important spiritual lesson that I have learned and taught for over forty years is a concept called "Spiritual Breathing." It is a simple way of understanding and pursuing the act of confession through the analogy of exhaling and inhaling. Millions of Christians around the world practice this revolutionary biblical truth.

First, *exhale*. Confess your sin to the Lord. Agree with God that your thoughts or actions have displeased Him. Then thank Him, on the basis of Christ's death on the cross, that He has forgiven you of your sin. Be assured that because God is merciful, He will always forgive your sins if you sincerely confess them. "But if we confess our sins to Him, He is faithful and just to forgive us and to cleanse us from every wrong " (1 John 1:9).

Second, *inhale*. Surrender your life once more to the Lord. Ask Him to fill you with His Holy Spirit. Ask Him to strengthen you so that your inner attitudes and outer actions will keep you from falling into the same sin again.

Think for a moment about how your body needs to breathe. When you exhale, you are ridding your lungs of carbon dioxide and other impurities that would cause disease if they stayed in your system. Then, when you inhale, you breathe in the oxygen that is crucial for maintaining a healthy body. So it is with spiritual life. When we sin, our fellowship with God is broken. That is why we feel distant from God, and become complacent and discouraged. But through Spiritual Breathing, we can enjoy renewed fellowship with God and experience the abundant life He promises.

Steps to Being Filled with the Holy Spirit

Having considered the obstacles to submitting ourselves to Him, we can turn to the question of how you and I can experience the wonderful filling of the Holy Spirit. Just how can that wonderful event come to pass in our lives? I believe there are several essential steps. Let us examine them in order.

1. Desire to be controlled and empowered by the Holy Spirit.

I had been a believer for two years in 1947 when I traveled to Forest Home, a retreat center in California, to be the dean of a junior high conference. Dr. Henrietta Mears, my spiritual mentor and the dynamic director of Christian education at First Presbyterian Church of Hollywood, had just returned from Europe and at chapel time gave a passionate plea to help take the gospel to a needy, desperate world.

After chapel, she, William Evans, Jr. (the son of our pastor), and I were meeting together and were suddenly enveloped with the presence of the Holy Spirit. We were intoxicated with the joy of His presence. I remember falling to my knees, overcome with a sense of His glory and majesty. I had the feeling that, if I could not praise Him, my heart would burst. William has said that he felt as though coals of fire were moving up and down his spine.

Into the room came Richard Halverson, a defeated, frustrated minister who was ready to resign his ordination and go back to pursuing an acting and singing career in Hollywood. But the moment he entered the room, he too was transformed by the presence of the Holy Spirit. God called all of us that night to a whole new dimension of holiness, power, and grace.

As a matter of record, Dr. Richard Halverson went on to become one of the leading ministers in America as well as chaplain of the U.S. Senate. William Evans, Jr. became the outstanding pastor of many U.S. presidents through the National Presbyterian Church in Washington, D.C. Dr. Henrietta Mears continued her fruitful ministry and had a powerful impact on the lives of multitudes. Many of us, including Billy Graham, could say that there are few people who have had a greater impact on our spiritual lives than Dr. Mears.

Do you sincerely desire to be controlled and empowered by the Holy Spirit? Listen to the words of the apostle John:

> Jesus stood and shouted to the crowds, "If you are thirsty, come to Me! If you believe in Me, come and drink! For the Scriptures declare that rivers of living water will flow out from within." (When He said "living water," He was speaking of the Spirit, who would be given to everyone believing in Him. But the Spirit had not yet been given, because Jesus had not yet entered into His glory.) (John 7:37–39).

Are you hungry to know your Lord in a deeper, more meaningful way? Are you thirsty to have a relationship with the Lord that is more intimate than you ever thought possible? Then come to the Lord and drink. Drink deeply of His Holy Spirit and know life more abundant and fulfilling than you have ever known before. You need only ask Him. He is overjoyed when His children come with this request, and He is quick to fill us with His Spirit.

2. *Confess all disobedience to God.*

As mentioned earlier, sin short-circuits our fellowship with God. It pollutes our prayers and deadens our ability to hear His voice.

In 1952, as Vonette and I were beginning our ministry at UCLA, she was troubled by an experience from college. Every time she prayed to be filled with the Holy Spirit, the Lord would remind her of this college experience. As we discussed her concern, it seemed to me to be an extremely minor issue. My advice was to ask God for forgiveness and move on. But Vonette saw the issue as deeper, something she needed to resolve. She wrote letters to the people involved in that situation and offered her apology. Immediately there was something different about Vonette's life. The evidence? The next fifty young women she talked to at UCLA received Christ. God was sending us a message through that incident that we would never forget. Vonette simply obeyed God, confessed the sin in her life, and acted on her repentance. As a result, the Holy Spirit filled her and produced an incredible harvest through her ministry.

Confess to the Lord whatever sin may be in your life. Always ask the Holy Spirit to reveal those unrealized sins, the ones that fly beneath our spiritual radar. Prayerfully ask the Holy Spirit to show you the areas in your life where changes are required. List these areas of disobedience on a sheet of paper. Then agree with the Lord about the nature of the items on your list: they are sins. Accept the forgiveness you have received through Christ's death on the cross.

Then repent. As an act of your will, make a choice not to continue these unhealthy patterns in the future. Ask the Holy Spirit to enable you to fulfill your commitments. Burn the paper with its list of your sins. This will help you realize that just as the flame destroys your list, so God promises to erase from His memory *all* of your sins.

The Bible states this wonderful promise: "If we confess our sins to Him, He is faithful and just to forgive us and to cleanse us from every wrong" (1 John 1:9). Every sin that you and I have ever committed and will ever commit has been paid for with the precious blood of our Savior. Jesus canceled all of the charges against us. We are forgiven for all time.

Confess your sin, apologize to those you have wronged, repent, reconcile, and experience the joy of Christ's forgiveness. If you do that, you will enjoy the same power for life and ministry that Vonette and I have experienced for more than fifty years.

3. Surrender control of every area of your life to our Lord Jesus Christ.

For most Christians, this is usually the major obstacle. There is always some area of their lives that they are unwilling to turn over to Christ's rule. It may be finances, relationships, work, friends, or something else. But it is usually something that they feel they cannot possibly give up. That area will keep them from knowing the sweet joy, peace, and excitement of being totally surrendered to our Lord. I have believed and trusted God for more than fifty years, and He has never disappointed me—only blessed me.

Listen to the words of the apostle Paul as he admonished the believers in Rome to give themselves completely to the Lord:

> And so, dear brothers and sisters, I plead with you to give your bodies to God. Let them be a living and holy sacrifice—the kind He will accept. When you think of what He has done for you, is this too much to ask? Don't copy the behavior and customs of this world, but let God transform you into a new person by changing the way you think. Then you will know what God wants you to do, and you will know how good and pleasing and perfect His will really is (Romans 12:1,2).

The very God who created and controls over 100 billion galaxies and all they contain is the very One who loved you and me when we were dead in our sins. He loved us enough to send His Son, the Lord Jesus Christ, to earth as a human being, conceived by the Holy Spirit and born of the virgin Mary, to be crucified for us. You can trust Him with every area of your life.

How about your love for the Lord? Do you truly love Him enough to trust Him with the whole picture—every aspect of your life? Think about each of the major areas of life: work, goals, family, relationships, habits. Which is the hardest for you to trust to God? This question is a test of no less than your love for Him. We trust those whom we love.

4. Ask God to fill you with the Holy Spirit.

If you have let go of all the areas of life you were withholding from God, and if you have surrendered complete control to Him, then you need only make this wonderful request: simply ask the Holy Spirit to fill you. By faith, thank God for filling you with His precious Spirit.

Just as you were saved by faith, you will be filled by faith. By faith you will live in His presence and His power moment by moment. Salvation was made available to you by your simple, childlike faith in what Christ did for you on the cross. At that time the Holy Spirit came to dwell within you. Being filled by the Spirit works much the same way: you simply trust the Spirit to fill you completely. As you surrender to Him, He will gladly take control.

By the power of the Holy Spirit, God is molding His children into the likeness of His Son.

So many wonderful things will begin to happen in your life after that moment. You will know Jesus Christ as you have never known Him before. You will discover His exciting and challenging will for your life. And because it is what He has created you to do, you will be eager and happy to fulfill it. You will experience the intense joy of fellowship with Him every single day, wherever you go and in whatever you do. You will wonder why you did not allow the Spirit to fill your life long, long ago—and you will no longer be hesitant to share your faith with non-believers on a daily basis, because you will want others to experience the same joy you are experiencing.

If you have not been filled with the Spirit before, I cannot imagine any excuse you might have for delaying another instant. I suggest that you use the following prayer to surrender yourself totally to God and allow His Spirit to fill you completely:

Dear Father, I need You. I acknowledge the fact that my life has been a hopeless pattern of sin and disobedience against the loving and gracious plan You had for me all along. I thank You and praise You for forgiving my sins through Christ's death on the cross for me. And now, at this watershed moment of my life, I invite Christ to again take His rightful place of authority on the throne of my life. Nothing will be held back. I give it all to You. Fill me with the Holy Spirit as You commanded me to be filled, and as You promised in Your Word that You would do if I asked in faith. I now thank You for directing my life and transforming me into the kind of person You created me to be.

5. Expect the Holy Spirit to work in and through you regardless of how you feel.

If you have met the above conditions and have, by faith, asked the Holy Spirit to fill you—rejoice! The work has been done. Now you can expect the Spirit to work in and through you even when you feel nothing special.

I have already spoken briefly on the issue of unreliable emotions. As we have seen, our faith is based on the facts of God's inspired Word rather than our feelings.

At times you may feel as if you are full to bursting with the love and joy of the Holy Spirit. But there may also be times when you will feel as if you are in the lowest valley. If so, you may wonder if the Holy Spirit is on vacation—or if all this business about His filling was just your imagination in the first place. Take comfort. These are simply the ups and downs of our moods. Regardless of how we feel, God is working out His perfect will in us and through us whenever we allow Him to do so.

By the power of the Holy Spirit, God is molding His children into the likeness of His Son. Each day that goes by, we should endeavor to have more of Christ and less of our old, sinful natures. You can expect to experience a growing pattern of victories as you face trials and struggles through Christ's strength. You can expect to feel more peace as you are confronted by crises. The Holy Spirit, as He fills your life, will be teaching you, comforting you, redirecting you toward higher and higher planes where you can be of ever greater service to God.

Things that may be powerful temptations to you today will become much easier for you to withstand as you mature. Pastor and author R. Kent Hughes says it well:

Where the Spirit reigns, believers relate to the Word—teaching.
Where the Spirit reigns, believers relate to each other—*koinonia.*
Where the Spirit reigns, believers relate to God—worship.
Where the Spirit reigns, believers relate to the world—evangelism.[3]

The Holy Spirit impacts with great blessing every person, church, or family He inhabits and controls. Being filled with the Spirit is an experience that brings unspeakable joy and delight to the human soul. Expect to see your life change in remarkable ways as you are filled with the power and presence of God's Comforter.

Life Application

 Meditate on the Words of the Spirit. Commit the following verses to memory:

- "Those who obey My commandments are the ones who love Me. And because they love Me, My Father will love them, and I will love them. And I will reveal Myself to each one of them" (John 14:21).

- "Blessed are those who hunger and thirst for righteousness, for they shall be satisfied" (Matthew 5:6, NASB).

 Focus on the Presence of the Spirit. Search your heart as you ask the following questions:

- Do you have any doubts or reservations about being filled with the Holy Spirit?

- Have you developed any habits or patterns of sin? Will you repent of these and do whatever is necessary—make restitution, ask forgiveness, seek outside help—to stop sinning in this area through the power of the Holy Spirit?

- Are you willing to give every area of your life to God and put Him in charge of your life—completely?

Pondering these questions prepares you to be filled with the Holy Spirit. Do not worry if you struggle in certain areas. We all do. Just give those areas to God. Only He can give you the strength you need to honestly face your struggles, seek forgiveness, and live a Spirit-filled life.

 Walk in the Power of the Spirit. Pray the following prayer if you are ready to invite the Holy Spirit to fill you.

Awesome Creator God and Savior, thank You that You long to live Your life in and through me. What a privilege! I desire, with all my heart, to be controlled and empowered by Your

Holy Spirit. I confess my sin to You. [Take time to list specific sins.] I give You every area of my life: my spouse, my children, my work, my dreams, my health, all of my possessions. They are Yours! Fill me with Your Holy Spirit. Thank You for working Your plan through me. Please remind me that no matter how I feel, Your Holy Spirit is living Your life through me as I become Your hands, Your feet, and Your heart to others around me. Thank you. To You be all glory! Amen.

Part Two

An Intimate Presence

Chapter 4

Our Teacher of Truth

I f you've ever visited an amusement park, perhaps you found yourself wandering into a Hall of Mirrors. It is quite a disorienting experience. On every wall is a mirror, but the mirrors are sloped, twisted, and angled to create distorted reflections.

I think we could all agree that while the Hall of Mirrors might be an amusing place to visit, we would rather not live there. Unfortunately, we do live in a world of twisted and distorted views. On the day Adam and Eve rebelled against God in the Garden of Eden, sin first made its way into the world. It has done its work of destruction ever since. Sin might be described as the force that twists all the "mirrors" out of shape. It shows us only grotesque views of what God created to be beautiful.

Sin has corrupted everything. We have no point of reference—unless we begin to see life from a godly, biblical perspective. That is one function of the Holy Spirit. In this world, we cannot trust our own impressions. We need judgment; we need a dependable authority. The Holy Spirit is with us at all times, whispering in our ears. If we can learn to hear His voice, we will have a Guide who never fails.

Even with the presence of the Holy Spirit in your life, you still have a free will, and can be willful and disobedient. You can choose to give in to temptation and reap the sad consequences. Then, the next time temptation comes along, you will find it much easier to ignore the still, small voice of the Spirit and give in again. This is what we call a "slippery slope."

Why Are We So Easily Deceived?

One might think that common sense alone would be enough to keep us out of trouble. It should be easy enough to see that giving in to a particular temptation would be bad for the health; giving in to another specific one would destroy the marriage. Yet people make tragically poor decisions every day. I believe there are four reasons why most people are deceived so frequently in life.

The first is the matter of *who is doing the deceiving*. The Bible tells us that the chief prince and ruler of this world, Satan, is the Master of Deception. "Satan, the god of this evil world, has blinded the minds of those who don't believe, so they are unable to see the glorious light of the Good News that is shining upon them" (2 Corinthians 4:4).

The enemy has been practicing his craft since the dawn of time, and he understands which approaches are most likely to succeed. The devil works overtime, trying to distort every truth we have received from God. He makes ugly things seem beautiful and foolishness seem wise.

Keep in mind that after the experience of salvation, our souls are under God's protection.

Keep in mind that after the experience of salvation, our souls are under God's protection. Nothing Satan could devise can snatch us from the security of our heavenly Father's grip. The war is over, but spiritual battles and skirmishes continue to rage all around us. Satan wants to convince you that he has not been defeated. He cannot take away your eternal life with God, but he can cause you great misery on this earth and harm your testimony for our Lord. He still has the ability to draw you away from the victorious, abundant life you were created to enjoy.

A second reason for our deception also involves the Great Deceiver. *Satan's lies can be more difficult to detect because he mixes in just a pinch of truth.* Half-truths are far more deceptive than outright lies. In the garden, the devil actually quoted God's Word; he did the same when he was in the wilderness with Jesus. But as always, he twisted and misrepresented the truths of God's holy Word. Always keep in mind that he will give you "good," often "spiritual" reasons to do the wrong thing.

A third reason it is difficult to see through the world's false reality is because *sin distorts our reasoning and judgment.* This is like wearing smudged eyeglasses—or, in biblical terminology, "we see things imperfectly as in a poor mirror" (1 Corinthians 13:12). It is not only the "mirrors" which lie to us, but also our very reasoning faculties are corrupted. This is why it is so important for us to pray and seek God's guidance on issues large and small; we cannot trust our flawed human judgment.

A fourth reason for our deception is that *the basic values of the world, which are so opposed to God's values, are held before us so many times that they become persuasive.* The world constantly praises the immediate, while the Bible speaks for the eternal. The world exalts the self, while the Bible exalts Christ. The world glorifies materialism, while the Bible extols spiritual values.

Our only safe harbor from this deluge of untruth is the truth of God's Word. If we stray away from it, we will quickly fall prey to the world's delusions. Praise God that He gave us His holy, inspired, inerrant Word. But how does He use it in our lives?

How Does God's Word Make a Difference?

When it comes to finding our way in a strange city, road maps are essential. We often trust our own fallible senses of direction, only to find it more than worthwhile to unfold that road map which we have ignored.

God provided His Word so that we would have a road map for navigating our way through a complex and dangerous world. What a wonderful thing to realize that we have access to the very teachings and principles that guided God's people thousands of years ago—and to know that His Word is eternal and never changes. Peter wrote, "Above all, you must understand that no prophecy in Scripture ever came from the prophets themselves or because they wanted to prophesy. It was the Holy Spirit who moved the prophets to speak from God" (2 Peter 1:20,21).

The Scriptures give us—in sixty-six books of history, poetry, prophecy, and wisdom—a thorough picture of God's laws, love, and character, as well as case studies of His way of dealing with people. As the Spirit brings light to these words for your life, you will learn more about God than in any other way.

It is no wonder that nonbelievers are puzzled by our allegiance to the Book; they have no Holy Spirit living within them to illumine and apply the words to their lives. But Christ sent the Holy Spirit to guide us into all truth. He does that in many ways, but the most basic of them all is through His Word. The day you became a Christian, the scales fell from your eyes regarding the holy Scriptures. Up to that point, you could expect to receive no more blessing from those pages than any other nonbeliever might. They consider it little more than an ancient book. Although the Scriptures provide "the wisdom to receive the salvation that comes by trusting in Christ Jesus" (2 Timothy 3:15), the lost see little value in it regarding daily wisdom for life.

The day you accepted Christ, all that changed. The Spirit came into your life, and He opened your eyes to see *into* Scripture with true understanding. Over and over you will hear believers say, "The words really jumped off the page for me!" It is a living Word that we read and cherish. Time and again the Spirit will use the Word to shed light on the issues of your life.

Note the Bible's careful definition of itself: "All Scripture is inspired by God and is useful to teach us what is true and to make us realize what is wrong in our lives. It straightens us out and teaches us to do what is right" (2 Timothy 3:16). What a wonderful description. The Word, through the interpretation of the Spirit, is fully interactive with our daily lives. It shows us the path and keeps us close to it.

In short, the Bible is the ultimate road map. Please read it, study it, memorize it, and meditate upon it each morning and throughout the day, until your last conscious thought each night.

How Does the Spirit of Truth Teach Us?

As Jesus dined with the disciples in the upper room during that final Passover, He offered them a preview of things to come. He told of the coming of the Spirit, who would continue the work that Jesus had begun. "When the Spirit of truth comes," He said, "He will guide you into all truth. He will not be presenting His own ideas; He will be telling you what He has heard. He will tell you about the future. He will bring me glory by revealing to you whatever He receives from Me" (John 16:13,14). In other words, the Spirit comes with a focused agenda. He brings God's Word and plan to you. He equips you for the future that lies ahead.

But what are His methods for imparting truth to us? The well-known English pastor Charles Spurgeon (1834–1892) suggested three distinct strategies. The Holy Spirit, he observed, employs *suggestion*, *direction*, and *illumination* in order to show us truth. I find this a helpful pattern for studying the ways of the Spirit. Let us examine each one.

Suggestion. Have you ever had a thought cross your mind out of the blue, one that seemed entirely distinct from your normal thought processes? Such notions could come from almost anywhere, of course, but we need to be aware that the Spirit will often place thoughts into our minds. There might suddenly be a powerful notion to pray for a specific individual. We might find that the perfect words are suddenly in our mouths as we share our faith. We think, "I had no idea I could be that eloquent!" We cannot, of course—but the Spirit can.

Obviously, we need to be careful about what we credit to the Spirit. We can certainly be misled about the source of an idea. This is why it is so important to take "every thought captive to the obedience of Christ" (2 Corinthians 10:5, NASB). We need to use wise discernment and "test the spirits" to be certain that we are correctly recognizing God's voice.

Direction. In suggestion, a single thought stands out in the mind as if it appeared from nowhere. But there are other times when a chain of thoughts seems to be carefully guided in the direction that God would desire.

The Holy Spirit is capable of directing our thoughts in a particular line of reasoning that produces new insight and new understanding of the truth. Direction does not involve implanted words, but a guided stream of thought. You smile in the knowledge that God's Spirit has redirected your thinking to just where He wanted it to go.

"'My thoughts are completely different from yours,' says the LORD. 'And My ways are far beyond anything you could imagine. For just as the heavens are higher than the earth, so are My ways higher than your ways and My thoughts higher than your thoughts'" (Isaiah 55:8,9).

Illumination. Earlier in this chapter, we explored the way the Spirit works in our lives in regard to the Word. A good word for that is *illumination.* Who better to interpret the Scriptures than the very One who inspired them? There is a crucial New Testament passage that gives us more information about the Spirit's illumination:

> The wisdom we speak of is the secret wisdom of God, which was hidden in former times, though He made it for our benefit before the world began. But the rulers of this world have not understood it; if they had, they would never have crucified our glorious Lord . . . But we know these things because God has revealed them to us by His Spirit, and His Spirit searches out everything and shows us even God's deep secrets . . . But people who aren't Christians can't understand these truths from God's Spirit. It all sounds foolish to them because only those who have the Spirit can understand what the Spirit means (1 Corinthians 2:7–15).

You have something the world will never have—until it turns to Christ. The greatest wisdom of the age seems to make no sense at all unless illumined by the light of the Holy Spirit. Jesus said, "He will bring Me glory by revealing to you whatever He receives from me" (John 16:14). Jesus has a word for every day, every moment, and every issue of your life. He will offer it to you through the wonderful ministry of the Holy Spirit.

How Do We Cooperate with the Spirit of Truth?

You may have observed the following fact in any classroom: Some students make excellent grades while others fail, even though the teaching was the same for both. Most of the difference is in a student's attitude toward learning. In the same way, the amount you will learn from the Spirit of Truth is based not on His performance—He is available equally and fully to all believers—but on your cooperation and teachability as His student. There are several things you can do to become an "honors student" under the Holy Spirit.

Trust the Holy Spirit to teach you. It all begins with faith. The apostle John offers the highest of recommendations:

> But you have received the Holy Spirit, and He lives within you, so you don't need anyone to teach you what is true. For the Spirit teaches you all things, and what He teaches is true—it is not a lie. So continue in what He has taught you, and continue to live in Christ (1 John 2:27).

We would be very foolish not to trust the Spirit to teach us and not to be the best possible students.

I challenge you to be proactive about claiming this powerful truth. That is, ask the Spirit of Truth to teach you all that He has for you. Dedicate yourself to listening, learning, then living. Make that request and covenant with Him today.

Revel in God's truth by hearing, reading, and memorizing the Word of God. It is comforting to realize that we have the Spirit's basic textbook. A great deal of what He has for you to learn has already been recorded in the Scriptures. You need to be diligent in the study of God's Word every single day of your life. In time, you will not be able to imagine doing anything else, so powerful will be the positive impact of His Word in your life.

Make sure you have a worthy translation of the Scriptures, one with good notes. Keep a notebook with your Bible, so you can write down all that you learn as it comes to you. Work regularly at Scripture memorization. You may initially be hesitant to do this kind of work, but we always memorize the names, faces, numbers, and details that matter to us in life. An investment of a few minutes each day memorizing a verse of Scripture will pay great spiritual dividends for the rest of your life. The Spirit will be able to fill your heart and mind with the Word of God, wherever you may go. There is power in the Word, and your life is entirely different when the Word becomes the soundtrack of your life.

Even at eighty years of age, I still memorize Scripture and draw regularly on verses that I memorized over fifty years ago. There is no material treasure that can compare with the Scripture you hold securely in your heart and the promises of God, which you can claim for all occasions.

Uncover God's will by meditating on the truths He has revealed in His Word. There is an art to meditating on the Word of God, and it takes some time to cultivate such an art. We are more accustomed to reading for information. That is important, but we also need to take time to let the Word simply soak into our hearts and minds.

Reflection and meditation go much deeper than the kind of reading most of us do. We must attempt to dig deeply into the Scripture passage, understand it as thoroughly as possible, and discover what the Spirit might be saying to us through it. Ask these kinds of questions: What does it say? Is there a command for me to follow? Is there a promise for me to claim?

God, who has revealed Himself to us in three Persons, is one, and the Holy Spirit is the third Person of that Trinity.

Listen for the Holy Spirit's application of the passage to your life. Be sensitive to what He is saying and to His instruction. He may illuminate a verse so that it suddenly comes alive and seems to jump off the page into your heart as never before. He may also provide a whole new understanding of a passage you have read many times before. When we read the Word, we should never say, "Yes, I have read this verse before; I will move on." We must listen anew for what the verse says about our life here and now.

It has been my joyful privilege to read through the Bible each year. I find it to be fresh, stimulating, and inspiring daily.

Test the insights to be certain they are from God. This is a point we must never forget. We are cautioned to "test everything that is said. Hold on to what is good" (1 Thessalonians 5:21). Many terrible delusions have come from misapplication of Scripture. How can we know that we are hearing the voice of the Holy Spirit—the only Spirit of Truth—and not some other voice? I would suggest asking the following questions:

First, are your impressions consistent with Scripture? The Holy Spirit will *never* ask you to act in a manner that is in conflict with Scripture. The more you learn about God's Word, as you grow in your faith, the more you will be impressed with the consistency of the scriptural message. For example, God will never lead you to marry an unbeliever or to do anything dishonest.

Second, does the insight make sense? Satan suggested to Jesus that He should jump off the highest point of the temple in order to let the angels catch Him. Jesus knew His mission, and common sense indicated that this was not part of it. There are some decisions in life that you will not need to pray about. The good common sense that God gave you, controlled by the Holy Spirit, should be sufficient to help you make wise decisions.

Third, is the insight sensible in the light of circumstances? If you are deeply in debt but you want to buy an expensive new car, it is very unlikely that God is the one telling you to make the purchase. Remember that our God is not a God of disorder and irrationality.

Fourth, do godly pastors, teachers, and counselors agree with the impressions you have received? It is quite important to seek wise counsel. I have done this countless times in my life, and I hope you will do the same. Surround yourselves with wise, mature believers; they will provide a spiritual "safety net" to help protect you from a poor interpretation of God's will.

Finally, does the insight you have received generate deep, inner peace? This is the kind of peace the world simply cannot give. Running away from our circumstances may also generate peace—but only for a time. The kind of peace I am speaking of is not dependent on your circumstances. It is the supernatural peace that comes directly from God. If you are unsure of your interpretation and application of the Scriptures, look into your heart and determine whether you have the peace that comes from God.

Hasten to apply God's truth to your life. In the long run, of course, learning from the Spirit makes a difference in your life only if you act upon what you have learned. He teaches you not so that you will have more information, but so that you will have more impact.

If you refuse to act, the Spirit will finally stop teaching you. I know you will not make that mistake. As you learn something, you usually see quickly enough the reason why the Spirit taught it to you. No teaching is more practical than His teaching, and that will only spur you to listen even more attentively.

Open Our Eyes!

I would like to close this chapter with a favorite story from the Scriptures. It involves a prophet named Elisha who was filled with a zeal for serving God. One night, as recorded in 2 Kings 6, he was in the city of Dothan, surrounded by hostile forces from Aram.

Elisha had a servant who was very frightened. But his master said there was no reason to be fearful, for there were more warriors on God's side than the enemy's. This seemed like an irrational thing to say, for there were hordes of men, chariots, and horses outside the walls of Dothan. But Elisha prayed, "O LORD, open his eyes and let him see!" (2 Kings 6:17). And when the servant looked again, he saw that the surrounding troops were *also* surrounded—by horses and chariots of fire. There was a heavenly host that no one but Elisha had been capable of seeing.

Being taught by the Spirit means learning to see the invisible realities of life—your world from heaven's point of view. When others quake with fear, you will have a calm assurance of the sovereignty of God, even as you watch His hand at work. You can live and act with confidence and joyful assurance.

In the next chapter, we will discuss the intimate access we have to God as we explore how the Holy Spirit teaches us to pray.

Life Application

 Meditate on the Words of the Spirit. Make it a priority to memorize and meditate on the following verses:

- "You will know the truth, and the truth will set you free" (John 8:32).

- "When the Spirit of truth comes, He will guide you into all truth" (John 16:13).

 Focus on the Presence of the Spirit. Prayerfully answer these questions about your life:

- What do you value in life? Is that what God wants you to value?

- What wrong attitudes from the world have seeped into your thinking through the media, friends, or co-workers?

- Do you believe there are right and wrong answers to life's questions? Why do some people reject God's absolute standard for truth?

- What truth is the Holy Spirit revealing to you that you need to embrace wholeheartedly?

 Walk in the Power of the Spirit. The Holy Spirit longs to teach you God's truth. Commit yourself to the steps outlined in the following TRUTH acrostic so your mind and heart will be tuned to the wisdom of God.

Trust the Holy Spirit to teach you.

Revel in God's truth by hearing, reading, and memorizing the Word of God.

Uncover God's will by meditating on the truths He has revealed in His Word.

Test the insights to be certain they are from God.

Hasten to apply God's truth to your life.

One more reminder: Be sure to practice Spiritual Breathing, so you are always filled with and directed by your Teacher of truth, the Holy Spirit. Your old flesh is at war with God. As you surrender moment by moment to the Lordship of Christ, He will fight your battles for you.

Chapter 5

Our Helper in Prayer

Visualize the scene that opens Luke 11: Jesus is caught up in deep prayer, barely conscious of the disciples who have gathered to watch Him with fascination.

Imagine what those disciples saw, heard, and felt. Here was a man praying as no one had ever been seen or heard to pray. In those days, the Pharisees offered prayers that were public, pompous, and predictable. They mouthed a long stream of "vain repetitions," as Jesus called them. Prayer was a "town square" demonstration of one's religiosity. It was also one-way communication, for God seemed silent during this period; He had not powerfully spoken or dealt with His people since the time of the prophets. Prayer had become an empty, meaningless exercise.

But here was Jesus, who prayed at all times—who slipped away each morning for prayer, sought God in the midst of each important development, and seemed to have an incredible intimacy with His Father. This kind of prayer resembled a meeting with a beloved friend. So the disciples watched with fascination as He prayed in Luke 11:1. One of them could no longer contain his desire to experience something so wonderful. As Jesus finished praying, the disciple cried out, "Lord, teach us to pray!"

Have you ever felt like that? Have you commiserated with Ziggy, the cartoon character who stood on the mountain peak and called out to heaven, "Am I to be put on hold for the rest of my life?" All of us feel a deep craving not simply to talk to God, but to talk *with* God. We have no desire for the mere trappings of prayer; we want the real thing. And each of us has felt the disappointment of dry, dead prayer, in which our words seem to bounce off the ceiling and return to us unheard.

We read books on the subject. We try new methods. We wonder if there is some hidden formula or secret that will provide the key to powerful prayer. But in reality there is only one secret, and His name is the Holy Spirit. He carries us beyond our weaknesses and limitations. He carries us directly into the incredible, loving presence of God Himself.

How Prayer Brings Us to God

Prayer is the most intimate communication ever devised. It is heart to heart, spirit to Spirit communication between creation and Creator. It is talking with God: asking Him for guidance, praising Him for His goodness, sharing with Him the needs of ourselves and others, and knowing by faith that He hears and will grant our requests.

God longs to meet with us in prayer, because it represents the difference between truly *knowing* each other versus merely knowing *about* each other. You could spend your life studying the works of all the great theologians, and read every worthy Christian book ever written about God. You could become an expert on all the facts that have been revealed about Him. But still you would not *know* God, not even remotely, unless you communed with Him in prayer. A six-year-old girl who, with childlike faith, kneels at bedtime could know the Lord more intimately than you, for even her childish prayer is more intimate and personal than mere theological facts and doctrine. Real, living prayer is crucial, and it is only possible through praying in the Spirit.

As I live in the Spirit, prayer is the foundation of my day and my way of life. As I awaken each morning, I invite the Lord to work in me and through me. I pray that everything that comes to my mind is filtered through the blood of Christ and the Word of God. And then I turn my thoughts to praise, prayer, and thanksgiving. What an honor to be able to bring our concerns to the One who made us and holds the universe together. As long as we can pray, there is hope in all things. If a family member is lost without Christ, prayer can make the difference. If a boss is overwhelming us with work, we have a place to take our concerns. If we are disappointed and heartbroken over a struggling marriage, we need never give up. We know there is always prayer.

Cherish this verse in your heart: "The effective prayer of a righteous man can accomplish much" (James 5:16, NASB). Intercessory prayer (praying for the needs of others), offered in a righteous spirit, can actually influence the course of history. It has happened many times in the past; in fact I believe it happens every day. In 1934, just to name one example, a farmer asked a group of his friends to come to his farm and spend the day in prayer. He was just an ordinary farmer. As the men prayed together, they felt compelled to ask God to raise up a man from their city to carry the gospel to the ends of the earth. There was no immediate answer. But the farmer's teenage son became a believer during the crusade that year. Although you would not recognize the farmer's name, you most likely have heard of his son: my friend Billy Graham.

That farmer was a world-shaker, because God answered his simple prayer. Never forget that you have every opportunity that farmer had.

How the Spirit Helps Us Pray

In the days when the temple was still in use in Jerusalem, only the high priest was allowed to enter the holy of holies to atone for the sins of the people—and this only once a year. When he entered that sacred place, he came into the very presence of God. An individual's closest encounter with God would be to interact with the priest, on the public side of the curtain.

Yet, as believers, now we can go past the curtain. We can approach the eternal, infinite Creator God of the universe any time of the day, any day of the year. Why? Because of the selfless sacrifice of our Savior Jesus when He died on the cross for our sins, we can "boldly enter heaven's Most Holy Place" (Hebrews 10:19).

The Spirit is the one who eagerly clasps your hand and walks you into God's throne room. "Now all of us, both Jews and Gentiles, may come to the Father through the same Holy Spirit because of what Christ has done for us" (Ephesians 2:18).

We should look upon prayer as the most precious, valuable privilege we could ever receive. We should take advantage of it at every available instant, and with eagerness: "So let us come boldly to the throne of our gracious God. There we will receive His mercy, and we will find grace to help us when we need it" (Hebrews 4:16).

The Spirit does a number of wonderful things to help us in our prayer life:

The Spirit prompts us to pray. Have you ever felt that little nudge? You may be going about your business, your mind on many earthly matters, when you sense a little mental tug. You feel the urge to pray about a particular matter or person. This impression could even wake you in the middle of the night. We hear of many Christians who, in various situations, were led to pray for a loved one or friend, only to find that this person was in a dangerous situation at that very moment.

Not long ago I felt a strong impression to pray for an outstanding man the Lord has used to impact 120 countries. I prayed for him only to feel yet another prompting, an urge to call my friend. So I dialed his telephone number. When I asked my friend how he was doing, he told me that it was the worst day of his life. He began to describe in detail the awful things that were happening to him that day. I tried to minister to his needs, sharing some similar experiences from my own life and how God had worked in the midst of them. Finally we prayed together.

At the end of the conversation, I could tell my friend had new strength and encouragement. He was amazed that I had called him at the very moment he needed encouragement. The Holy Spirit had used me to bring him comfort. I was glad that I had paid attention when the Holy Spirit had prompted me to pray for my friend. This has been my experience on numerous occasions.

The Holy Spirit guides our prayers. The Holy Spirit also molds and shapes our prayers, helping them to be effective and consistent with the will of God. He guides us through the needs of the day, through the emotions of the hour, and through recollections of people we care about. He helps us pray for all the many things we need to bring before the Father.

As He does this, something wonderful happens. The Spirit brings our desires into conformity with God's will. It may be that you have encountered a very difficult situation in life. You feel a great deal of anxiety, and naturally you ask God for a change in the circumstances. But as the days and prayers move by, you find that the circumstances remain the same while your attitude has utterly changed: you suddenly comprehend how God could use someone like you in just such a setting. You realize that He didn't want to help you *out* of this mess, but to help you *through* it. More miracles happen in the midst of a crisis than when we are fleeing from our circumstances.

God's Spirit guides your prayer over time, until you are asking for Him to lead you rather than remove you from the situation. The Bible assures us, "God is working in you, giving you the desire to obey Him and the power to do what pleases Him" (Philippians 2:13).

You pray for God to change things, but in the process, you are the one changed. It works much like the anchor on a ship. When men take hold of the chain to the anchor, their efforts pull the boat toward the anchor, rather than the anchor up to the boat. In the same way, when we pray, tugging at the "chain" of prayer pulls us toward God. We are moved gradually into His awesome presence where our hearts are transformed by the power of His love.

We should look upon prayer as the most precious, valuable privilege we could ever receive.

Prayer keeps you anchored in every sense of the word. When you feel the pull of the Spirit to turn your heart toward prayer, you can be joyful in realizing that you will be even closer to the wonderful purposes of God by the time you have finished.

The Spirit guides our prayer, and best of all He guides our spirits toward God.

The Holy Spirit intercedes for us in prayer. Here is one of the most remarkable promises and supernatural ministries of the Spirit in prayer. "In the same way, the Spirit helps us in our weakness. We do not know what we ought to pray for, but the Spirit Himself intercedes for us with groans that words cannot express" (Romans 8:26, NIV). I have always found this to be a tremendously encouraging concept. You may say, "But I lack the knowledge of how to pray!" Every believer should learn to pray biblically. However, that is not the major issue, because the Spirit prays for those things we lack the understanding to pray for. He also expresses the depth of emotion that we might feel if we could see with complete spiritual clarity. He helps us pray beyond our many limitations. Knowing this makes me all the more eager to pray, as I am sure it does you.

The Holy Spirit knows us better than we know ourselves. He understands our desires, our fears, our strengths, and our weaknesses. He knows what we need before we even know to ask for it. The Holy Spirit, the third person of the Trinity, knows the mind of God. "He who searches our hearts knows the mind of the Spirit, because the Spirit intercedes for the saints in accordance with God's will" (Romans 8:27, NIV). Who better to speak to our heavenly Father for us than the Holy Spirit?

We have so many limitations, so many failings. But we can be joyful in the realization that the Spirit of God stands in the gap, interceding for us. Your prayers are more powerful than you can possibly realize, because He enhances and enlarges them.

The Holy Spirit leads us in prayerful worship. Prayer, of course, is more than a flood of requests. The Spirit helps us to praise and exalt God when we pray. He gives us the realization of the awesomeness of God. He leads us to comprehend just how infinite, how majestic, and how sovereign He truly is, and then, as a result, we can do nothing other than worship in spirit and in truth.

The Spirit frees us from the monotony and dryness of dead prayer by filling our hearts with the wonderful music of true worship. Music begins where words leave off, and sometimes the only way to express our feelings about God's greatness is through the transcendence of melody and verse. Paul urges us, "Let the Holy Spirit fill and control you. Then you will sing psalms and hymns and spiritual songs among yourselves, making music to the Lord in your hearts" (Ephesians 5:18,19). The Spirit makes worship a natural and joyful thing, not merely at church but wherever we may be.

You will find that prayer is the spark that sets worship aflame. You may begin a devotional time with a mood nowhere close to that of worship. But then, as you praise your Lord for His many benefits, as you thank Him for all He has done in your life, as you realize all the many requests you are allowed to bring before Him—what can you do but exalt and magnify His name? You will break out in song within your heart, for words will not be enough. Then you will feel mentally, emotionally, and spiritually refreshed for having worshiped. The Spirit, in His wisdom, knew you needed that. So He became your worship leader.

In each of these ways, the Spirit makes the difference in our prayer. Now let us turn to some guidelines for praying in the Spirit.

How We Pray in the Spirit

We have seen some of the many ministries of the Holy Spirit in prayer. But how can we be caught up in the kind of prayer that allows us to sense the transforming presence of God? There are a number of considerations to remember.

We need to avoid certain common misunderstandings. Too often we feel that God is impressed by our verbal eloquence or the length of our prayers. He has no particular regard for either of these. A prayer from the heart, whatever the eloquence or length, is what He looks for. He wants us to pray in the very midst of our life and emotions. These are the times when we are likely to lift up the most heartfelt prayers.

Paul writes, "Pray in the Spirit on all occasions with all kinds of prayers and requests" (Ephesians 6:18, NIV). Your most effective prayers may come in the most unlikely places—though we never become so "informal" that we lose sight of the greatness and awesomeness of the One to whom we are praying. This brings us to our first suggestion for praying in the spirit.

Address God respectfully. To pray in the Spirit is to pray with a reverent heart. We should never come before God without reverence and awe. "Since we are receiving a Kingdom that cannot be destroyed, let us be thankful and please God by worshiping Him with holy fear and awe" (Hebrews 12:28). Fear is a word that is often missing today from our understanding of a relationship with God, but I believe it refers to a surpassing sense of how awesome and holy God is. When we come to grips with these realities, we are humbled, and God rewards the humble. The prophet Isaiah proclaimed, "The high and lofty one who inhabits eternity, the Holy One, says this: 'I live in that high and holy place with those whose spirits are contrite and humble. I refresh the humble and give new courage to those with repentant hearts'" (Isaiah 57:15).

We also feel joyfully thankful when we pray as the Holy Spirit leads. Do you spend as much time expressing gratitude as you do asking for more blessings? If not, this is a sign that you are not truly praying in the Spirit, who will usher you into God's presence and fill you with a thankful heart. You should have times of prayer that are completely given to thanking Him. The next time you cannot feel the presence of God, and you struggle to find an attitude of worship, spend some time expressing your gratitude. You will be amazed at how quickly your mood will change.

Initiate transparent conversation with God. Praying as the Spirit leads also gives us the freedom to be ourselves. As we have seen in James 5:16, "the effective prayer of a *righteous* man can accomplish much" (NASB, emphasis added). If we have confessed our sin, we realize there is no obstacle between God and us. We can be completely open and honest, telling Him exactly what is on our hearts. "If our conscience is clear, we can come to God with bold confidence. And we will receive whatever we request because we obey Him and do the things that please Him" (1 John 3:21,22). The key to answered prayer, then, is being in harmony with God. As we come into His presence and know Him more fully, that harmony occurs.

No relationship can be deep and strong without honest communication, and your relationship with God is no different. Wonderful liberation is experienced when we learn what it is like to be completely honest with God, with no shame or striving to be something we are not. We can worship Him "in spirit and in truth," as Jesus told the woman at the well (John 4:23). When you pray in the Spirit, you will be transparent with God. He knows all that is inside us anyway.

Speak to God as your Father, your dearest Friend. Speak simply and honestly with Him, telling Him the deepest concerns and emotions you are feeling. Open up with full transparency.

Declare your confidence in God. There is no need to come before God with hesitation and timidity, as if we lack trust in His power. We are praying to the Creator and Sustainer of the universe. If we are praying as the Spirit directs, we can confidently come before Him with our requests.

This means fully realizing our dependence upon Him. One of the most essential effects of prayer is the way it reminds us how helpless we are apart from Him. Each day we must submit ourselves to His lordship again, because our spirits are rebellious and stubborn. As we come before God, we acknowledge our limitations. We cast ourselves upon His mercy and His power, affirming that we can do no good thing on our own.

Then, having felt our own helplessness, we express faith in His worthiness. Praying as the Spirit directs strengthens our faith that though we are weak, He is strong. As we pray, we *believe*—we believe that He will act as He desires. We believe He will work through us. We believe that He is totally sovereign. Faith is strengthened when we pray in the Spirit, and we begin to live in the confident assurance that He is Lord, and that He is working in our world and through us. Praying in the power of the Holy Spirit always leads to greater confidence and hope in God.

In the matter of prayer, perseverance counts. Faith that God will act is not the same as faith that God will act today, tomorrow, or whatever my schedule may be. He wants us to pray without ceasing, to keep praying with persistence. He knows that the discipline of sustained prayer is good for us. We do not serve a God of convenience but a God of perfect timing—a timing we usually will not know in advance. Keep on keeping on as you pray in the Spirit with faith and endurance. Never give up!

God gave me a vision in 1945 to produce a film on the life of Jesus. The vision became a reality thirty-three years later. God gave me a vision to train world leaders. Twenty-five years later, that vision became a reality. Always keep on believing; God's timing is perfect.

How Prayer Reveals His Power

I believe the greatest revelation of God's power in the world comes through the vehicle of our prayer, as guided by the Holy Spirit. Prayer, often with fasting, accomplishes what nothing else will. It softens hearts. It calls friends and enemies to repentance. It reaches far beyond the borders of our mundane life to the other side of the globe and to generations yet unborn. It demolishes the devil's strongholds. Most important of all, it draws us into intimate communion with our awesome God. God is manifest in His magnificent glory through the prayer of His children.

There are so many true stories that illustrate the glorification of God and His power through the prayers of faithful believers that an entire library would be needed to contain them. Let me share one example.

I believe it is time for Christians to mobilize in prayer and put an end to a dead, dry prayer life.

In the mid 1800s, the great explorer David Livingstone feared for his life. As the sun set on his small camp in the interior of Africa, he knew the local tribe planned to attack that night and kill him and all of those by his side. Even in the midst of these warnings, Livingstone was strangely filled with peace. God was with him, and God could always be trusted. That night, Livingstone slept without anxiety—and his camp was unthreatened.

Two years later, a miracle happened: the chief of that hostile tribe became a Christian. Livingstone was eager to learn the story of why the tribe had never attacked on that memorable evening. The chief confirmed to him that an uprising had indeed been planned. They had left their settlement with weapons, anger, and the intent to kill. But as the tribe approached Livingstone's camp, they had been surprised by what they saw: forty-seven mighty warriors guarding the place where the famous explorer slept.

Livingstone was shocked to hear this story two years later, because he knew there had been no guards. What was the truth?

76

On a visit home to England, he found out. Livingstone was informed that on that night of crisis two years earlier, across the ocean in Scotland, forty-seven church members had gathered, drawn by the Spirit, to pray fervently for Livingstone. Those prayer warriors stood watch over Livingstone before almighty God, and his life was spared.

When people are caught up in the Spirit to pray before God, incredible things happen all around us. We release His miraculous power to a world that has forgotten how powerful God is. Forty-seven believers, deep in prayer, were enough to turn back a murderous attack. What would happen in this world if all of God's children became prayer warriors, available to the call of the Spirit to lift up His name and His purposes? How would your life change if you began to pray in the manner described in this chapter?

I believe it is time for Christians to mobilize in prayer and put an end to a dead, dry prayer life. Communing with God is the ultimate adventure, and it is available today, tomorrow, and every moment you live on this planet. Prayer begins and ends my day, filling it with faith and joy. I have seen the amazing power of God time and again because I prayed as the Spirit directed, and I know you can do the same. Can there be any better time than the present? What about this very moment?

As you complete the following Life Application page, I invite you to close this book and ask the Holy Spirit to direct your prayers. You will find yourself praying as you have never prayed before—prayer that avails much, prayer that transforms you and the world around you through the guidance and power of the Spirit. This kind of divine fellowship will begin to purify your entire life, which is the subject of our next chapter.

Life Application

 Meditate on the Words of the Spirit. Commit these verses to memory, and spend time reflecting upon their truth:

- "In the same way, the Spirit helps us in our weakness. We do not know what we ought to pray for, but the Spirit Himself intercedes for us with groans that words cannot express" (Romans 8:26, NIV).

- "Devote yourselves to prayer with an alert mind and a thankful heart" (Colossians 4:2).

- "Pray without ceasing" (1 Thessalonians 5:17, NASB).

 Focus on the Presence of the Spirit. Contemplate the following questions:

- Do you have difficulty finding time to pray, or pray only on the run? Why is this?

- Is there anything in your life—pride, unbelief, a wrong perspective of God, or any unconfessed sin—that is getting in the way of your prayers?

- What steps does God want you to take so you will have a prayer relationship with the Lord that is open, dynamic, and intimate?

 Walk in the Power of the Spirit. The Holy Spirit wants to help you develop an intimate prayer relationship with your heavenly Father. Commit yourself to practicing the truths in the AID acrostic so you can experience the power of Spirit-filled prayer:

Address God respectfully in prayer.

Initiate transparent conversation with God.

Declare your confidence in God.

When you pray today, ask of the Spirit what the disciples asked of Jesus. Ask Him to teach you to pray. Then be open to His guidance to experience the full and transforming presence of God.

Chapter 6

Our Motivator to Holiness

A t the beginning of the 19th century there lived a sculptor named Dannecker, one of the finest artists in the world. He specialized in carving images of Greek gods and goddesses. But Dannecker wanted to produce a true masterpiece—and he set his mind on sculpting a figure of Christ.

Dannecker's finished work was so beautiful that it brought gasps of admiration from everyone who saw it. Word of the new masterpiece finally reached the ears of the emperor Napoleon. "Come to Paris," he invited, through a message to the artist. "Carve me a statue of Venus for the Louvre."

The artist Dannecker politely replied, "Sir, the hands that carved the Christ can never again carve a heathen goddess."

Once we have touched those nail-scarred hands and looked into the eyes of the One who gave His life for us, we cannot live the old way any longer. When we have touched what is holy, we begin to look at all else in a completely different way. As committed believers, we resolve to live in a way that is clean, pure, and holy.

We must do our work for God in the darkness of this world. But while we are *in* the world, we can never again be a part *of* it. There are activities that must be left behind, habits we must break, and relationships we can no longer pursue. We know that our God has standards much higher than those of the world, and that our lives must begin to conform to them as closely as possible.

The Lord says to us, "You must be holy because I am holy" (1 Peter 1:16). Those words, of course, can seem intimidating to us. How can

81

we attain a holiness worthy of God? We realize immediately that we simply cannot, for we are prone to sin and failure. This is why Jesus came to die for us, even when we were yet sinners—because we had no hope of becoming worthy on our own. Yet the scriptural command remains, consistent and clear: we must be holy. We must lead lives of purity.

It seems a paradox, but we know our Lord would never give a command without affording us the provision for keeping it. How can we live in purity while we are surrounded by so much sin and temptation? The Holy Spirit is the answer.

Purity: The Goal of Holy Living

Holiness begins with the idea of separation—we have been set apart for a purpose. We are to maintain a distinction from the sinfulness of the world so that we might be dedicated to God. Our intention is to be as much like Him as humanly possible, and to share in His holiness. We are exhorted to "be imitators of God, therefore, as dearly loved children" (Ephesians 5:1, NIV).

God is our Father, and any doting father wishes to pass down the best character traits to his offspring. In a similar way, God desires to bestow His holiness upon us. He accomplishes this by being present, in all His purity and goodness, within us. Yet somehow we manage to forget something so wonderful, and Paul found it necessary to remind his friends at Corinth of this fact: "Don't you know that your body is the temple of the Holy Spirit, who lives in you and was given to you by God? You do not belong to yourself, for God bought you with a high price. So you must honor God with your body" (1 Corinthians 6:19,20).

Our bodies are, in the truest and most literal sense, temples of the living God. This requires purity in life. It means that our attitudes, motives, desires, actions, words, character, and lifestyle should proclaim the presence of our royal Guest. Paul instructs Timothy, his beloved spiritual "son" in the Lord, "If you keep yourself pure, you will be a utensil God can use for His purpose. Your life will be clean, and you will be ready for the Master to use you for every good work" (2 Timothy 2:21). This is the central idea of holiness: we strive to keep our lives as clean vessels, worthy of the miraculous presence of God that fills these earthly containers.

Purity is important to a silversmith. Yet he has no precise formula for knowing when his liquefied metal is pure. He simply recognizes that the silver is free of dross when he can see his reflection in the metal. You will know your life is pure when it reflects Christ with clarity. If your life is filled with impurities and "dross," how can your friends ever see the face of Christ reflected in it? In that regard, the mission of the Holy Spirit is to keep you separate from anything that would mar the image of Christ in us, including outright evil, as well as anything that dishonors God.

But it is extremely important to understand that the Holy Spirit does not sanctify our old nature. The Book of Romans tells us, "The old sinful nature within us is against God. It never did obey God's laws and it never will. That's why those who are still under the control of their old sinful selves, bent on following their old evil desires, can never please God" (8:7,8, TLB). It is impossible to take something old and decaying and make it brand new.

God is our Father,

and any doting father

wishes to pass down

the best character

traits to his offspring.

The "old man" that represents your former nature is dead, and he can never be rehabilitated. You began this life with that carnal, worldly nature that comes with your membership in the human race. But when you were reborn in Christ, the Holy Spirit gave your old nature the death sentence. Then He gave you an entirely new and clean life. Physically, we look exactly the same. Mentally, we have the same ability to choose as before. Emotionally, we may not feel a great deal of difference at times. But spiritually, it is the difference between life and death—both of those natures still live in conflict within you, the old, sin nature and the new, godly one. However, the old nature has been condemned and awaits final destruction when you finally come into God's full and unshielded presence at death; but it still attempts to distract and mislead you.

We need a deeper understanding here. What spiritual transactions occurred in your life when you placed your trust in Christ? In what sense were you reborn? How can the old self still have any influence?

How the Spirit Brings Holiness

Few believers realize how many spiritual events occur in that incredible instant when we invite Christ to be our Savior.

First and foremost, *we are liberated from Satan's grasp and reconciled to God.* The Bible explains, "For He has rescued us out of the darkness and gloom of Satan's kingdom and brought us into the Kingdom of His dear Son, who bought our freedom with His blood and forgave us all our sins" (Colossians 1:13,14, TLB).

Second, *we become brand new creatures.* Paul tells us this marvelous truth: "If anyone is in Christ, he is a new creation; the old has gone, the new has come!" (2 Corinthians 5:17, NIV). It is like wiping the slate clean and starting life all over again, in complete purity. All the perfection of Christ is attributed to us, though we have not merited this in the least. The Bible declares, "You were washed, you were sanctified, you were justified in the name of the Lord Jesus Christ and by the Spirit of our God" (1 Corinthians 6:11, NIV).

Here is a crucial point. Though these things have happened, and though we have been made completely new, we can still choose to listen to the destructive influence of the old self. *The Holy Spirit will be about His work, strengthening and sanctifying us to bring us closer and closer to the image of Christ.* But old habits die hard. The voice of the devil will still be in our ear, whispering enticements to do things the old, sinful way. And remember, the flesh is at war with God.

Throughout my Christian life, as I have faced temptations of many kinds, I have claimed the promise of 1 Corinthians 10:13, "No temptation has seized you except what is common to man. And God is faithful; He will not let you be tempted beyond what you can bear. But when you are tempted, He will also provide a way out so that you can stand up under it" (NIV). This promise is available to each of us in the war against sin. This is a daily battle, and through our victories over temptation, we will become stronger, wiser, and more holy.

Your life will not immediately become beautiful and sinless at the moment Christ comes to indwell you. But you will want a new kind of life that reflects Christ at its center. Everything in your life should point back to Him. You will be painfully aware of issues such as how you interact with people, what kinds of books and films you select, and how you spend your time. The Holy Spirit will show you everything in a new light. He will prod you to make changes, and He will give you the supernatural power to make those changes. You will face a work of daily renewal and renovation, but a satisfying one when you let the Holy Spirit do the reconstructing. You will be pleased with the new, upgraded life that results.

Take to heart the wonderful benediction Paul pronounces over you, God's cherished creation: "Now may the God of peace make you holy in every way, and may your whole spirit and soul and body be kept blameless until that day when our Lord Jesus Christ comes again. God, who calls you, is faithful; He will do this" (1 Thessalonians 5:23,24).

On the other hand, many Christians fail to make the right daily choices. Let us look at how sin corrupts us in our quest for holiness.

How Sin Brings Corruption

There is nothing complicated about the process of sin. We are tempted; we give in to the temptation; we act in disobedience to God; we reap the destructive consequences. But the ramifications are much more complex than this. Think of the ripples that result when a stone is tossed into still waters. Even a small sin creates "ripples" that have far-reaching consequences.

First, sin creates a barrier in your relationship with God. Could the Lord overlook our daily trifles of misconduct? No, for our Lord is a holy God. His standards are absolute purity and perfection. So He cannot look upon the slightest stain of sin, any more than light can co-exist with darkness or black with white. That obstruction must be removed or we will experience a blockage to our access to God.

The prophet Isaiah told his people, "There is a problem—your sins have cut you off from God. Because of your sin, He has turned away and will not listen anymore" (Isaiah 59:2). If we continue in our own selfish ways, God will turn His face from us, and we will quench the still, quiet voice of His Holy Spirit.

Sin affects not only our access to God, but our very perspective in life. Jesus said, "God blesses those whose hearts are pure, for they will see God" (Matthew 5:8). But when we disobey God's commands, we are blinded. We are unable to see with the clear vision that godliness brings. Sin can be like a tiny speck of dust in the eye that causes the vision to be blurry. "Without holiness no one will see the Lord" (Hebrews 12:14, NIV). It is impossible to keep our eyes on God while violating His laws.

In addition, there is the emotional issue of realizing that we bring grief to the Spirit within us. Paul tells us, "Do not bring sorrow to God's Holy Spirit by the way you live. Remember, He is the one who has identified you as His own, guaranteeing that you will be saved on the day of redemption" (Ephesians 4:30). We naturally want to please those we love, and causing them pain causes us pain. You will feel a deep sense of mourning when you know you have acted in disobedience to your loving heavenly Father.

We seldom realize how many people are affected by one act of spiritual disobedience.

Our sin brings pain not only to God but to others. This is another part of the ripple effect of sin—we seldom realize how many people are affected by one act of spiritual disobedience. An act of adultery disrupts two primary lives, but there are also family members, co-workers, friends, and other people who will eventually feel the spiritual and emotional turmoil of the sinful activity. The Bible assures us that the ripples extend down through entire generations; that the sins of the fathers are visited upon the children of their children. Sin may creep up silently, but it shouts across time and space.

Divorce is an example of a sin with tremendous ripple effects. We know that a vast majority of long-term prison inmates grew up with no father in the home. Girls from fatherless homes are far more likely to become pregnant before marriage. Drug abuse, poverty, and many other negative social forces are linked to poor home backgrounds. These poverty-stricken homes create a self-perpetuating cycle of even more poor homes, more crime, more drug abuse, and more misery. Sin produces terrible guilt and pain, which in turn causes future misery—unless the victims break the cycle through the redemptive power of Christ.

King David personally learned the devastation and destruction of sin. On a terrible impulse, he committed adultery with Bathsheba, then ordered the murder of her husband to cover it up. When he saw the tragic results he wrote, "For troubles without number surround me; my sins have overtaken me, and I cannot see. They are more than the hairs of my head, and my heart fails within me" (Psalm 40:12, NIV).

But David's story does not end there. The crushing guilt of his sin overwhelmed him until he came to God in repentance. "Have mercy on me, O God, according to Your unfailing love; according to Your great compassion blot out my transgressions. Wash away all my iniquity and cleanse me from my sin. For I know my transgressions, and my sin is always before me. Against you, you only, have I sinned and done what is evil in your sight" (Psalm 51:1-4, NIV).

Praise God that we need not live within the cycle of destruction. When we choose obedience and purity, we reap joy and abundance. God promises, "Those who live to please the Spirit will harvest everlasting life from the Spirit. So don't get tired of doing what is good. Don't get discouraged and give up, for we will reap a harvest of blessing at the appropriate time" (Galatians 6:8,9).

Why We Continue to Sin

There is everything to gain and only sorrow to lose when we live moment by moment in the purity of holiness. The choice is so clear, yet so many believers fail the test day after day, choice after choice. Why is this so?

For one thing, we make the mistake of attempting to live in purity through our own weak abilities and self-effort. It takes a supernatural enabling to live in constant victory when we are surrounded by the lure and temptations of the world. That ability is available only through the Holy Spirit. Paul wrote, "Let me ask you this one question: Did you receive the Holy Spirit by keeping the law? Of course not, for the Holy Spirit came upon you only after you believed the message you heard about Christ. Have you lost your senses? After starting your Christian lives in the Spirit, why are you now trying to become perfect by your own human effort?" (Galatians 3:2,3). Our own weakness brought us to God in the first place, and it is a great mistake to continue living in that weakness. Yet most believers do.

At the same time, many of us sin because we fail to realize our true nature. Let this verse saturate your mind: "Our old sinful selves were crucified with Christ so that sin might lose its power in our lives. We are no longer slaves to sin. For when we died with Christ we were set free from the power of sin" (Romans 6:6,7). After the American Civil War, all slavery was outlawed. Those who had lived as slaves were completely free. But tragically, there were many who were not told. They continued to live and toil in bondage because they had no knowledge that a new life was possible. We, too, often fail to realize the truth of our emancipation. Christ has truly set us free. We need not live in servitude to the devil. The time has come to shake off the chains and begin a new life.

There is also the problem of simply giving in to the desires of the old sin nature. We fall into those old sinful patterns. Paul explains the impulses that still sadly control some of us:

> I advise you to live according to your new life in the Holy Spirit. Then you won't be doing what your sinful nature craves. The old sinful nature loves to do evil, which is just opposite from what the Holy Spirit wants. And the Spirit gives us desires that are opposite from what the sinful nature desires. These two forces are constantly fighting each other, and your choices are never free from this conflict (Galatians 5:16,17).

The old sin nature still tugs at us, and the world encourages it. The Bible tells us in 1 John:

> Do not love the world or anything in the world. If anyone loves the world, the love of the Father is not in him. For everything in the world—the cravings of sinful man, the lust of his eyes and the boasting of what he has and does—comes not from the Father but

from the world. The world and its desires pass away, but the man who does the will of God lives forever (1 John 2:15–17, NIV).

The devil, of course, is always at work through the world and the old sin nature that is still within us. We should never forget that he will use every clever strategy to make the world and its sin seem attractive. Because each day is fraught with temptations that he will place in our paths, we need to daily put on our spiritual armor and stand firm. Every believer should regularly meditate on the sixth chapter of Ephesians, especially the following portion:

> Be strong with the Lord's mighty power. Put on all of God's armor so that you will be able to stand firm against all strategies and tricks of the devil. For we are not fighting against people made of flesh and blood, but against the evil rulers and authorities of the unseen world, against those mighty powers of darkness who rule this world, and against wicked spirits in the heavenly realms (Ephesians 6:10–12).

There is one final but very crucial reason why we continue to sin. We lack a reverential fear of God. If we truly comprehended the greatness and sovereignty of God, if we understood His absolute purity and holiness, if we could grasp how He abhors and punishes sin, we could not possibly remain stubborn in our disobedience.

Our God is loving and full of grace. He is gentle and forgiving. But it is equally true that "our God is a consuming fire" (Hebrews 12:29), and that "it is a terrible thing to fall into the hands of the living God" (Hebrews 10:31). The Creator and Sustainer of the universe has the power to give life or to snatch it away. Life is fragile, like a mist, and we owe every breath to Him. We need to realize that He must, as a part of His just and holy nature, punish sin for what it is: an affront to His purity.

If you were to spend five minutes each day in silent contemplation of the awesome majesty and absolute justice of God, would you continue to sin frivolously? I believe that if each of us will come to grips with His incredible attributes, we will live with a wholesome fear of God. We will live, through the enabling of the Holy Spirit, with more purity and holiness than we ever thought possible.

How We Can Break the Sin Cycle

How then shall we live?

To live for self is to be consumed with self-absorption. It will set us immediately at odds not only with God but with all other people including ourselves. We will be led to break God's laws and to break ourselves upon them. Only misery, sorrow, and tragedy can result.

However, living for Christ will place us under the influence of the Spirit of God, who will guide us with love and grace. We will live to please God and others, therefore finding wonderful fulfillment and peace for ourselves. In the meantime, we will be constantly about the work of purification, keeping our lives as clean vessels for the shining presence of God. Paul encourages us, "Let us purify ourselves from everything that contaminates body and spirit, perfecting holiness out of reverence for God" (2 Corinthians 7:1, NIV).

You can break the cycle of sin and sorrow by doing several things:

Perceive your position as a new creation in Christ. You may not feel righteous. You may think God still condemns you for past sin. But in truth, you have been freed from sin and death by Christ's own death on the cross. The Spirit of God lives within you. When the Father looks at you, He sees all the righteousness of His dearly beloved Son. "God made him who had no sin to be sin for us, so that in him we might become the righteousness of God" (2 Corinthians 5:21, NIV).

Uproot your sinful nature by faith. Since Christ was put to death for you, you must put your old self to death for Him. "Those who belong to Christ Jesus have nailed the passions and desires of their sinful nature to His cross and crucified them there" (Galatians 5:24). God wants us to crucify the old, corrupted person we once were.

Forgiveness and salvation comes once, but the execution of the sinful nature is a daily, moment by moment event. We need the Holy Spirit to give us strength, wisdom, and resolve in continuing to experience victory over the old sin nature that once controlled us. It would rise yet again from its grave and regain control over our actions. But the presence of the Spirit provides all the power we need to enable us to resist yielding to temptation.

Resist sin and Satan's temptations. Temptation may seem severe, but it is only a test. The Lord will never allow Satan to tempt you beyond what you are able to endure. He will always provide you with a way out. The promise of 1 Corinthians 10:13, which I referred to earlier in this chapter, should be a life-line to cling to when temptations arise.

By memorizing and claiming this promise, I have been saved from thousands of temptations, which had I yielded to would have destroyed my spiritual life and ministry.

When Satan sees his strategy fail, what does he do? Wander off? Drift into the shadows? No, he *flees*—and what a glorious moment of victory that is. Our standing up to the devil in the power and might of the Holy Spirit puts the fear of God into him. The Bible promises, "So humble yourselves before God. Resist the devil, and he will flee from you" (James 4:7).

Imitate godly behavior. Little children learn by imitating their parents. Believers learn in exactly the same way—by emulating the godly behavior of others. Paul told the church in Corinth, "Be imitators of me, just as I also am of Christ" (1 Corinthians 11:1, NASB). John, too, spoke of imitation: "Dear friend, do not imitate what is evil but what is good. Anyone who does what is good is from God. Anyone who does what is evil has not seen God" (3 John 11, NIV). It is important to have uplifting models. Just as your children need them, so do you. Mentors can be very helpful as role models for godly behavior. And, of course, Jesus Himself is the ultimate model.

Think holy thoughts. But what kind of holy thoughts? Paul counsels us to immerse our minds in all that is worthy: "Fix your thoughts on what is true and honorable and right. Think about things that are pure and lovely and admirable. Think about things that are excellent and worthy of praise" (Philippians 4:8). We are surrounded, however, by the very opposite. Television and magazines will fix your thoughts on all that is false and dishonorable.

But it is an essential Christian discipline to control the environment of your imagination. Your thoughts and values change when exposed to pornography, violence, and other sinful activities. Even spending time with cynical, sarcastic people will have its effect upon your perspective. Advertisers spend billions of dollars each year on the proposition that images and sensory information can change your mind and behavior. Because we know this is true, we must strive to expose ourselves to good and worthy influences at every turn. Take care what ingredients you pour into your mind.

Yield to the Spirit's control. Let Him empower you daily to walk in all of God's ways. Ask Him moment by moment to guide you and keep you from evil. Scripture assures us, "Live by the Spirit, and you will not gratify the desires of the sinful nature" (Galatians 5:16, NIV).

I do not wish to test the laws of the spiritual realm any more than I want to test the law of gravity.

It is dangerous and destructive to live in our own self-centered, limited strength and understanding. To do so makes us vulnerable to decisions that can destroy our spiritual life and witness. I live in reverential fear of God and do not wish to test the laws of the spiritual realm any more than I want to test the law of gravity by jumping out of a window in a tall building.

You Can Live a Life of Purity

If by chance you are afraid to approach Him because of the sin in your past, you need to be freed of those shackles. Guilt is the cruelest and most domineering of masters. You may be shaking your head and saying, "God would never embrace me; He knows my wicked past. He knows how I have lived. He knows the places I have gone and the things I have done. He could feel nothing but disgust with my life." If this is how you feel, you have not fully understood and reckoned with the perfect grace, compassion, and forgiveness that God has to offer. He has already forgiven every one of your sins. He loves you no less than He did on the day He created you, and now He longs to heal your troubled spirit.

In the next chapter we will look at the comforting work of the Spirit in the midst of our pain.

Life Application

 Meditate on the Words of the Spirit. Commit the following verses to memory:

- "Be imitators of God, therefore, as dearly loved children" (Ephesians 5:1, NIV).

- "Therefore, if anyone is in Christ, he is a new creation; the old has gone, the new has come!" (2 Corinthians 5:17, NIV).

 Focus on the Presence of the Spirit. Search your heart as you ask the following questions:

- What would your life look like if the Holy Spirit was given free access to "renovate" your heart and life for Christ?

- With what aspects of your life or personal habits do you know God is not pleased?

- What do you think is keeping you from confessing these wrong attitudes or actions and turning away from them?

 Walk in the Power of the Spirit. You cannot, through your own best self-effort, overcome the powerful temptation of sin. The Holy Spirit alone can free you from destructive habits, attitudes, and addictions and mold you into the image of Christ. Commit yourself to the truths outlined in the PURITY acrostic and start moving today toward a holy lifestyle.

Perceive your position as a new person in Christ.

Uproot your sinful nature by faith.

Resist sin and Satan's temptations.

Imitate godly behavior.

Think holy thoughts.

Yield to the Spirit's control.

Today, ask the Holy Spirit to shine a searchlight on every aspect of your life. Ask Him to show you the impurities that need to be cleaned away, as well as any obstacles to the holy and pleasing life He would like you to lead. Ask Him to strengthen you to begin a new life today—a life pure and powerful in its commitment to God's standards.

Chapter 7

Our Comforter in Adversity

Life is difficult. We find it to be unpredictable, challenging, and often brutal. We shake our heads as we see innocent people abused and dishonest people prospering. The world does not seem to play by the broadest rules of fairness and justice. I am certain that somewhere on the road of your own experience, you have discovered this truth in the most painful of manners. We can only rest in the assurance that God has a purpose for all the adversity He allows in our lives.

In such times we can afford to be reminded that suffering refines our character. There are things we cannot learn, virtues we cannot gain through any path other than the crucible of suffering. Young children must learn certain things the hard way, as we have all observed. We can tell them what is right and what is wrong, but there is no more powerful teacher than experience. Life works the same way, on a different level, for the rest of us. We need to learn patience, and we can only learn it through the agony of waiting. We need to learn forgiveness, and we can only develop it when there is something difficult to forgive.

Suffering is never welcome but nearly always useful. When we undergo some painful affliction in life, our first question is, "Why should I have to experience this?" I would suggest to you that this is the wrong question. A better one would be, "What is God trying to teach me through my suffering?" We will never know why bad things happen, but we can discover what good things can emerge from them. Affliction is often the messenger of God's deepest truths.

When any kind of fine metal is being refined, impurities must be burned away. When we feel pain in life, we can look upon it as our own period of refinement. We can remember that we are on the way to becoming God's pure and strong metal, ready to serve Him. As a matter of fact, we can go beyond even patience and acceptance. The Bible tells us that suffering is an opportunity for nothing less than joy.

> Dear brothers and sisters, whenever trouble comes your way, let it be an opportunity for joy. For when your faith is tested, your endurance has a chance to grow. So let it grow, for when your endurance is fully developed, you will be strong in character and ready for anything (James 1:2–4).

Have you ever looked upon trouble as a time for joy? This is not foolishness but the deepest kind of wisdom. This joyful perspective is the very key to persevering and growing in wisdom during times of affliction. We look at our feet and see not a stumbling block but a stepping stone. This is a necessary stop on the way to a life that is useful to God. It is the way to deeper understanding through the fires of experience. It is the way to being able to comfort and counsel others. Tears may come, but they should be tears not only of pain but of hard-won joy.

It has been said that we as Christians are like tea bags: we are not much good until we have gone through a bit of hot water. When the temperature rises, we learn something about ourselves and about God. We find out that we need a little seasoning, and that He is steadfast and faithful in our trials. You might learn many things about God simply by reading them in a book such as this one; but you will learn far more deeply and more powerfully through your own experience. Can you trust God? I must tell you that you can, but your faith will never be real until you are forced, through circumstances, to place all your trust in Him. Listen to what God said to Israel through the prophet Isaiah:

> When you go through deep waters and great trouble, I will be with you. When you go through rivers of difficulty, you will not drown! When you walk through the fire of oppression, you will not be burned up; the flames will not consume you (Isaiah 43:2).

Two years ago I was diagnosed with pulmonary fibrosis and told there was no hope of recovery. Yet God has filled me with His peace and is doing something wonderful in my life. Since I received the news that the world would consider terrible, God has actually found new uses for me. He has focused my limited energy on some of the greatest opportunities I have ever encountered. I have had more time to devote to books such as this one, and to numerous video projects that I could not have done in my previous busy schedule. I have been able to help launch the Global Pastor's Network, whose goal is to train millions of lay pastors to plant five million house churches around the world using the *JESUS* film and other ministry tools.

Our loving God is so creative and resourceful. Where we see limitations, He sees unlimited opportunity. He finds great joy in bringing the greatest miracles from the harshest conditions.

More Reasons for Suffering

We suffer for more reasons than just the need for refinement, of course. It is also true that we bring about affliction through our own disobedience. Any good parent will punish a child who misbehaves. We call this discipline, and it occurs in the spiritual as well as the physical realm. Undisciplined children—we have all known a few—grow up to face confusion and hardship. Their parents have not properly prepared them, through discipline, for the realities of the world.

In the same way, God must discipline us because He loves us, even if that means hardship and suffering at times. Affliction is often a "wake-up call," dramatically drawing our attention to the poor choices we have made. We learn a lesson we will not need to relearn. In wisdom we understand that God has punished us because He loves us. God Himself tells us, "My child, don't ignore it when the Lord disciplines you, and don't be discouraged when He corrects you. For the Lord disciplines those He loves, and He punishes those He accepts as His children" (Hebrews 12:5,6).

Whatever the reason for our suffering, we find that it offers an opportunity to draw closer to God. Some individuals who are disciplined become bitter, while others become better. It is always a matter of attitude and free will. Think of the experience of Job, the godly

97

character of the Old Testament who suffered more pain and anguish than we can possibly comprehend. He lost all his livestock, all his children, and even his health. His wife sat beside him in his suffering and bitterly suggested, "Curse God and die!" His "friends" told him he must be a very bad person to merit so much of God's judgment. Yet through his suffering, Job gained an incredible intimacy with God, who became very real and present to him. In the end Job could say, "Though He slay me, yet will I trust Him" (Job 13:15, NKJ), and, "My ears had heard of You but now my eyes have seen You" (Job 42:5, NIV).

Though it may be difficult to believe at times, suffering glorifies God and points the way to future glory as well. As Peter wrote:

> Dear friends, don't be surprised at the fiery trials you are going through, as if something strange were happening to you. Instead, be very glad—because these trials will make you partners with Christ in His suffering, and afterward you will have the wonderful joy of sharing His glory when it is displayed to all the world (1 Peter 4:12,13).

Christ's suffering culminated in His crucifixion. But beyond the cross of pain lies the victory of the open tomb. Beyond death lies resurrection. And beyond whatever suffering may be your lot, you will find "the wonderful joy of sharing His glory when it is displayed to all the world."

Even so, as we await a future that justifies our suffering, there is comfort for the present. How do we find this comfort?

How the Spirit Comforts Us

The disciples must have trembled in fear in that upper room as Jesus told them He would be leaving. What would life be like without the Master? Yet Jesus told them He would not leave them alone; He would be sending them a Comforter. The word He used is translated as Comforter, Counselor, Encourager. These are all services we perform for a hurting person. It has the meaning of someone who is called alongside, to help in times of trouble.

The Holy Spirit is the One who comes to us with tender comfort and encouragement, but who also brings power and strength. He is the ideal companion when we are beset by misery and grief. He knows us deeply, intimately, better than we know ourselves. He knows exactly what kind of encouragement we need, and He has the power to strengthen and heal us. In times when we feel incapable of expressing the depth of our pain, we know that He understands.

It is a wonderful truth to contemplate: we need never again be alone. Where could you go to escape the companionship of the Holy Spirit? What pain could you feel that He would not understand and comfort? I hope you will remember that wherever you are, whatever trial you may be facing, the Comforter is right there beside you. Perhaps you remember the film *The Hiding Place* from some years ago. The book and the film tell the story of my dear friend Corrie ten Boom and her sister, Betsy, who were sent to Ravensbruck concentration camp because they protected Jewish people during World War II. One night several women were gathered around Betsy as she led a Bible study. One of them suddenly spoke up bitterly. "If your God is such a good God," she said, "why does He allow this kind of suffering?" She slowly opened her hands to reveal broken, beaten fingers. "I'm the first violinist of the symphony orchestra. Did your God will this?"

Though it may be difficult to believe at times, suffering glorifies God and points the way to future glory.

Corrie looked sadly at the woman's hands. "We can't answer that question," she said with compassion. "All we know is that our God came to this earth, became one of us, suffered with us, and was crucified and died. And He did it for love."[1]

Power and Peace

God's love for us is deep and personal. Through His Spirit, He enters into the places of our pain and performs a work of healing that cannot be matched. Only He is capable of bringing joy, strength, and endurance in the face of the worst of calamities. All across the world we hear stories of believers under persecution. In many countries, Christians are pursued and punished, even put to death. And yet it is in these very settings that we discover great miracles occurring. Believe me, representatives of Campus Crusade's International Ministry department bring us new and breathtaking stories all the time. It would take another book for me to recount even a fraction of them.

Such incredible power in the face of affliction is not possible through any human agency or reserve, but only through the supernatural power of God's Spirit. He loves us with an everlasting love, and He fills us with an everlasting comfort. The power comes from knowing and living out what Paul wrote to the Romans:

> I am convinced that nothing can ever separate us from His love. Death can't, and life can't. The angels can't, and the demons can't. Our fears for today, our worries about tomorrow, and even the powers of hell can't keep God's love away. Whether we are high above the sky or in the deepest ocean, nothing in all creation will ever be able to separate us from the love of God that is revealed in Christ Jesus our Lord (Romans 8:38,39).

They can take away all our possessions. They can even take away our physical life. But they can never take away the most precious attainment we have, which is our living relationship with God. To know that is to be empowered.

Along with that power comes peace. Dietrich Bonhoeffer, a German scholar and theologian, denounced the Nazis as evil and became a potent voice in the German resistance. He knew the Nazis would not tolerate him for long, but he was a servant of Christ and believed God wanted him to minister to His people in Germany no matter what the cost.

In 1943, the Nazis arrested Bonhoeffer and incarcerated him in a Nazi concentration camp. On a Sunday morning, after leading a worship service, he was hanged. The camp's liberation by the Allied forces was only days away, but not in time to save Bonhoeffer's life. As he was being taken to the gallows, the scholar remarked to an English prisoner of war, "This is the end, but for me the beginning of life."[2] Where can that kind of peace be found? Only one place: the indwelling presence of the Holy Spirit.

Any believer who walks in the Spirit should enjoy that kind of peace. And no believer should ever be controlled by anxiety, for an overmastering anxiety is a symptom of being out of step with the Spirit. Paul, who lived in prison with the prospect of execution, wrote, "Don't worry about anything; instead, pray about everything. Tell God what you need, and thank Him for all He has done. If you do this, you will experience God's peace, which is far more wonderful than the human mind can understand. His peace will guard your hearts and minds as you live in Christ Jesus" (Philippians 4:6,7).

Life will always have its worries, but we have a place to go with them. The Comforter reminds us that the victory has already been won, and we can face the worst that life has to offer. "Here on earth," Jesus said, "you will have many trials and sorrows. But take heart, because I have overcome the world" (John 16:33). It does not matter if the entire Roman army is arrayed against us. It does not matter if the powers of Hollywood, Madison Avenue, and the media oppose us. It does not matter if our bosses, coworkers, and neighbors are negative toward Christ. It is only Christ whose opinion matters. He has overcome the world, and He promises believers that all our pain will ultimately be used for our good (Romans 8:28).

Comfort from Fellow Believers

The Holy Spirit also sends other comforters. One of the wonderful things that God does through our pain is to draw us closer to our fellow believers. We are reminded just how much we need them and how incomplete we are on our own. Have you ever watched geese fly south for the winter? By flying in their famous "V" formation, the birds fly 71 percent farther than if they flew independently. The beating wings of the lead flyer create an updraft for the goose directly behind it. Then, when the lead flyer tires out, it drops back and a fresher member of the flock takes its place.

Sick or wounded geese fly inside the "V," where there is the least wind resistance. The others help an ailing goose if it is forced to land. Two other geese follow the sick one down, nursing and protecting their fallen comrade until it either recovers or dies. Only then do they fly off.[3]

God teaches us a lesson through those geese. When we stand together, we are far greater than the sum of our parts. We care for our sick and wounded through the church. We watch and wait for God to send us to someone who particularly needs us. And God will often place someone who needs you right in your path. You will speak to someone at work or receive a phone call from an old friend. That little prompting in your spirit will tell you, "This is a time for ministry. The Lord wants me to help and encourage this person."

You should also expect God to send comforters when you are the one who needs comfort. Some Christians are prideful about accepting help. They have learned this not from the Bible but from the world, which teaches independence and self-sufficiency. There is no reason you should suffer in solitude; there is every reason to let your trial become an opportunity to draw closer to other believers. Ask for help and prayer when you need it. Let other Christians minister to your needs. God desires to bless us through fellow believers helping one another.

There is no reason you should suffer in solitude. Ask for help and prayer when you need it.

As you face those trials, and as you draw closer to other believers, rest also on the mighty promises of God. I cannot tell you just how much these powerful words have sustained me through times of ill health. Have you taken time to study God's promises? Doing so will greatly bless your heart. We cling to the wonderful claims of Scripture because we know that God has never once failed to honor them.

We seldom realize the incredible extent to which God wants to bless us through these promises. At any time we are invited to claim one and soak in the blessing that comes through it. For example, the Lord promises to . . .

> sustain all who fall,
> be near to all who call upon Him,
> fulfill the desire of those who fear Him,
> keep all who love Him,
> execute justice for the oppressed,
> give food to the hungry,

set the prisoners free,
open the eyes of the blind,
raise up those who are bowed down,
support the fatherless and widows,
heal the brokenhearted
(Psalm 145:14,18–20; 146:7–9; 147:3, NASB).

Those verses offer a handful of amazing promises, but I assure you they are merely the tip of the iceberg. There are literally hundreds of promises in Scripture, and each one is life-changing. When you need comfort, go to the Word and seek out these comforting promises.

As you study the Scriptures each day, one of the questions you should ask is, "What promise is here for me to claim?" I challenge you to begin making a list of them. Claim them for your own, and keep a record of how God proves faithful to His promises. Abundant living is the result of trusting in the cherished promises of God.

Cooperating with the Holy Spirit in Adversity

The Spirit is our Comforter, and He is always with us in every time of trial or grief. But this comfort is not something we accept passively. We need to be proactive in cooperating with the Spirit as He helps us. There are several actions that will enable you to experience the comforting strength of the Holy Spirit in difficult times. Let us discuss them.

Cast your cares on God. The Bible says, "Give all your worries and cares to God, for He cares about what happens to you" (1 Peter 5:7). Do you know what it means to sign your anxieties over to the Lord? I will tell you how to do that.

Next time you feel overwhelmed by your worries, go to a place of solitude. Perhaps you can sit beneath a leafy tree somewhere, with nature all around you. Take pen and paper with you and write God a letter. Tell Him in the letter that you realize you are incapable of holding the position of chairman, president, and CEO of your life; you hereby resign and offer those positions to God. From now on, you pledge to let Him supervise all the operations of You, Inc. State that you need not lose another minute's sleep in worrying about the challenges of life. God is in charge; this is His operation from now on. Sign your letter and post it somewhere you will see it often.

Sometimes we need an uplifting little ceremony like that just to help us understand the reality of truly casting our cares upon Him. As long as we believe we are in this alone, we will never feel true comfort. Assigning your anxieties to the Lord is an essential discipline.

Offer yourself for God's use in the midst of hardship. When we face adversity, either we can become self-absorbed and completely focused on our problems, or we can turn our eyes to selfless ministry. Paul, in reflecting upon his own suffering, wrote, "I am willing to endure anything if it will bring salvation and eternal glory in Christ Jesus to those God has chosen" (2 Timothy 2:10). You will find in all his letters that as he faced trials and disappointments, Paul turned himself more and more to serving his many friends in the body of Christ. As you face trials, redouble your commitment to serve God in the midst of them.

Meditate on God's promises. Let me stress once again the power of claiming God's promises. These are the richest and most exciting truths known to humanity, and the best time to reach for them is when we need comfort. I advise every Christian to compile a list of favorite promises from God's Word, memorize them, and keep the list available at all times. Wallets and purses are good places for them, and you can keep them on your refrigerator or in your place of prayer as well. I have a stack of twenty-five verses, which are laminated and available to memorize a few minutes here and there. One of the greatest blessings of my life has been claiming and experiencing the reality of these promises. I encourage you to memorize as many of God's promises as possible, so that the Holy Spirit may bring to your mind the perfect promise at just the time you need it. "Trust Me in your times of trouble," says the Lord, "and I will rescue you, and you will give Me glory" (Psalm 50:15).

That trust will be bolstered by claiming any of the multitude of promises found in the Scriptures. Here is one to start you out, a verse that will afford you untold comfort in tough times: "Do not be afraid or discouraged, for the LORD is the one who goes before you. He will be with you; He will neither fail you nor forsake you" (Deuteronomy 31:8). Is this not the perfect time for you to commit this verse to memory?

Face your trials with the assurance of victory. C. H. Spurgeon often declared he was so sure of his salvation that he could grab onto a cornstalk, swing out over the fires of hell, look into the face of the devil, and sing, "Blessed assurance, Jesus is mine!"[4]

Throughout my years of ministry I have spoken frequently about the importance of being solidly assured of our salvation. In the same way, we can claim victory over anything the devil may be throwing in our path. Is there any way the schemes of Satan can be successful in the face of God's power? Not if we claim the victory through Christ. Our victory as believers is assured not because of good works, but because at the cross Jesus Christ triumphed over Satan, the world, and sin. The war itself has been won, and we must face these lingering skirmishes with full assurance. Paul writes,

> That is why we never give up. Though our bodies are dying, our spirits are being renewed every day. For our present troubles are quite small and won't last very long. Yet they produce for us an immeasurably great glory that will last forever! So we don't look at the troubles we can see right now; rather, we look forward to what we have not yet seen. For the troubles we see will soon be over, but the joys to come will last forever (2 Corinthians 4:16–18).

Occupy your mind with positive thoughts. Hold a coin in your hand and you will agree that you can view only one side at a time. Suffering is a kind of coin that is paid out to everyone. If you are going to view one side, choose the victorious one. Look closely at the side whose inscription reads, "And we know that God causes everything to work together for the good of those who love God and are called according to His purpose for them" (Romans 8:28). Study the image on this side of the coin—the image of Christ that we are coming to resemble more every day through the power of the Spirit, and in the wisdom and endurance that comes through our suffering. Hold this coin tightly in your hand, for it will help to purchase a future of maturity and assurance.

These are some of the positive thoughts that should control your mind when you are being tested. Paul suffered as much as any of us, and he turned every tear to joy. He wrote these words: "We can rejoice, too, when we run into problems and trials, for we know that they are good for us—they help us learn to endure. And endurance develops strength of character in us, and character strengthens our confident expectation of salvation" (Romans 5:3,4). I believe that if you comprehend this truth, you will learn to face your trials with a positive mindset.

Remember God's faithfulness. Do you remember Jesus' story of the shepherd who leaves his ninety-nine sheep to search for the one that is lost (Luke 15:3–7)? There is also a small arctic sea bird called a guillemot. It lays its eggs side by side with countless other guillemots on narrow, rocky ledges in the far north. All the eggs look exactly alike, but if one is moved, the mother will notice. She will search for her egg until she finds it, then she will return it to its original location.[5] How much more faithful is God than a shepherd or a bird? He will never leave you nor forsake you.

Because Christ lives in us through His Spirit, we are to maintain an attitude of thanksgiving at all times.

Peter writes, "So if you are suffering according to God's will, keep on doing what is right, and trust yourself to the God who made you, for He will never fail you" (1 Peter 4:19). In other words, trust and obey, for there is no other way. Put your trust in the faithfulness of God, and obey Him in your actions as you await the victory that will come through adversity.

Thank God in the midst of your difficult circumstances. When times are good, give thanks. When times are bad, also give thanks. When times are somewhere in the middle, give thanks. Because Christ lives in us through His Spirit, we are to maintain an attitude of thanksgiving at all times. Paul wrote, "No matter what happens, always be thankful, for this is God's will for you who belong to Christ Jesus" (1 Thessalonians 5:18).

I believe you will find that even during the most difficult trials, there will never be a time when you cannot think of a wide assortment of blessings for which to be thankful. Indeed, the trials themselves present occasions for thanksgiving. We can say, "Thank You, Lord, for the things you will teach me from this experience. Thank You for the wisdom I will store up in the school of suffering. Thank You that, although I do not fully understand why I am facing these hardships, I fully understand that You can be trusted, and that everything I encounter will be used for my good."

You will be amazed at how your frame of mind will change simply by thanking God. He will honor you for your steadfast faith. The Holy Spirit will bring you comfort and encouragement, and you will feel a "second wind" to run the race and claim victory at the finish line.

Victory at the Far Side of Suffering

On July 30, 1967, a teenager named Joni Eareckson Tada was paralyzed in a diving accident. She completely lost the use of her arms and legs. How would you expect a teenager to deal with such tragedy? What kind of mindset would you predict?

I will allow Joni herself to answer:

> Only God knows why I was paralyzed. Maybe He knew I'd ultimately be happier serving Him. If I were still on my feet it's hard to say how things might have gone. I probably would have drifted through life—marriage, maybe even divorce—dissatisfied and disillusioned. When I was in high school, I reacted to life selfishly and never built on any lasting values. I lived simply for each day and the pleasure I wanted—and almost always at the expense of others... [Now] I wouldn't change my life for anything. I even feel privileged."[6]

Here is a Christian who has walked through the valley of suffering and emerged with a feeling of privilege. She is not crazy, and she is not deluding herself. She is like Peter, Paul, and all Christians who have counted it an honor to be held worthy of suffering for the glory of God. There is comfort in seeing how God works and uses our pain. There is comfort for our souls that comes through the ministry of the

Holy Spirit. There is comfort in knowing what rewards await us when we enter into the presence of Christ after this life.

No one is eager to suffer, but we should never be overcome by our misery. After all, we serve the ultimate Overcomer, and He will comfort and strengthen us, and use us for purposes greater than we can imagine. I will leave you with one final promise in this chapter: "You can be sure that the more we suffer for Christ, the more God will shower us with His comfort through Christ" (2 Corinthians 1:5).

In the next chapter, we will consider the person and ministry of the Holy Spirit as peacemaker.

Life Application

 Meditate on the Words of the Spirit. Make it a priority to memorize and meditate on the following verses:

- "Dear brothers and sisters, whenever trouble comes your way, let it be an opportunity for joy. For when your faith is tested, your endurance has a chance to grow. So let it grow, for when your endurance is fully developed, you will be strong in character and ready for anything" (James 1:2–4).

- "Don't be afraid, for I am with you. Do not be dismayed, for I am your God. I will strengthen you. I will help you. I will uphold you with My victorious right hand" (Isaiah 41:10).

 Focus on the Presence of the Spirit. Prayerfully answer these questions about your life:

- What hardships are you currently facing?

- How have these difficulties affected your relationship with God? Have you struggled to see God's goodness in the midst of your hardships?

- Have you given your struggles to God?

- How does the Holy Spirit want you to confront your problems?

 Walk in the Power of the Spirit. The Holy Spirit is called the Comforter. He longs to hold you and comfort you with His peace and love, if you will only let Him. Purposefully practice the following steps in the COMFORT acrostic:

Cast your cares on God.

Offer yourself for God's use in the midst of hardship.

Meditate on God's promises.

Face your trials with the assurance of victory.

Occupy your mind with positive thoughts.

Remember God's faithfulness.

Thank God in the midst of your difficult circumstances.

Chapter 8

Our Peacemaker in Conflict

All around us there are wars and rumors of wars. It has always been that way, and always will be until our Lord returns. By now it should be clear that humanity will be at war with itself as long as it remains at war with God. Only in Him is there peace; apart from Him there can be no future but one of turmoil and tragedy.

The only effective peace agreement is the one written in Christ's blood. It cleanses us of all the strife that consumes us in our struggles with God and one another. Paul wrote to the Ephesians, "For Christ Himself has made peace ... by making us all one people. He has broken down the wall of hostility that used to separate us" (Ephesians 2:14). Only godly individuals and nations, of course, will know the kind of peace Paul is describing. We are the soldiers who mobilize to spread the wonderful gospel of Christ's liberation all over the world. We are the soldiers who fight in the knowledge that our victory is already secure.

Peace is a wonderful ministry of the Holy Spirit, who knits believers tightly together. I believe most Christians fail to realize just how much emphasis is placed upon our peace and unity in the New Testament. Jesus said, "My prayer for all of them is that they will be one, just as You and I are one, Father—that just as You are in Me and I am in You, so they will be in Us, and the world will believe You sent Me" (John 17:21).

Unified by One Body and One Spirit

Only the Holy Spirit can banish the barriers dividing the human race
—nationality, race, economics, politics, age, or sex—and mold our
hearts together. If the Spirit is truly guiding us, we cannot help seeing
that such barriers have come down: "There is one body and one Spirit
—just as you were called to one hope when you were called—one
Lord, one faith, one baptism; one God and Father of all, who is over
all and through all and in all" (Ephesians 4:4–6, NIV).

We were not called to divisions or differentiations among believers,
but to one Lord, one faith, and one baptism. Our God deeply desires
us to experience the unity of being one body—the body of Christ. Too

We were not called to divisions or differentia-tions among believers, but to one Lord, one faith, and one baptism.

many of our churches, as I am certain you
have observed, dissipate their energy in all
kinds of divisions based on worldly standards such as wealth or age. The Spirit calls
us not to divide ourselves but to combine
our love and our gifts toward unity with all
true believers. When was the last time you
crossed economic barriers to minister to
someone who needed help? I pray that you
will let the Spirit guide you in those directions.

We are not only one body, but one Spirit.
The baptism of the Holy Spirit creates a mar-
velous unity that surpasses all manmade boundaries. A pastor who
has ministered for many years to believers in the People's Republic of
China reports that the Communist government is extremely fearful of
Christians. Why? Because of their unity. Through the power of one
Spirit, believers transcend the national boundaries of China. They are
believers first and Chinese nationals second. This means the Chinese
government cannot properly control them, a fact the government finds
frightening.

When we realize there is one Holy Spirit among us, we begin to
see the foolishness of getting caught up in quarrels. Is the Spirit within you different than the Spirit within your fellow believers? That
Spirit would never encourage a fracture of any kind within Christ's

112

fellowship. He seeks to knit you together in love. If you or your church become bogged down in conflict, perhaps you need to discover whether you are in step with God's Spirit.

Bonded in One Hope and One Faith

We also have unity in the manner of our hope. How do you live with hope in a hopeless situation? Christians from the former Soviet Union could speak to this question.

Kozlow, a criminal who later became a Christian, wrote about life in a Soviet prison. He and other prisoners cursed each other, the institution, and those who ran it. They lived in a miniature universe of bitterness as they struggled to endure the cruel, inhumane conditions. "We opened up our veins or our stomachs, or hanged ourselves," reports Kozlow. "[Yet] the Christians (often with sentences of twenty to twenty-five years) did not despair. One could see Christ reflected in their faces. Their pure, upright life, deep faith and devotion to God, their gentleness and their wonderful manliness became a shining example of real life for thousands."[1]

What made the difference? Why did the nonbelievers take their own lives while the believers were able to rise above their circumstances? *Hope.* The believers knew they had an eternal life and a reward that could not be taken away. They knew that the Spirit of God was among them. This is a hope that is all-encompassing, a hope that is infinite. Within each of us it should endure and become so overwhelming, so compelling that the world cannot help responding. Who could possibly bear a brighter hope? Ours outshines ten thousand suns, for it originates with the One who created them: "Praise be to the God and Father of our Lord Jesus Christ! In His great mercy He has given us new birth into a living hope through the resurrection of Jesus Christ from the dead" (1 Peter 1:3, NIV).

We share one hope because we share one Lord. We are diverse, no matter how strong our unity. We come in many nationalities, and we worship in many styles. But the Lord our God is one God. As I have traveled throughout the world over the past fifty years, I have observed that the moment I am with other believers, we know we are brothers and sisters because of our mutual love for our Lord. Our clothing, our culture, our language, and our customs may differ, but the Lord who binds us together is one and the same. He does not change. Paul explains this glorious truth: "But we know that there is only one God, the Father, who created everything, and we exist for Him. And there is only one Lord, Jesus Christ, through whom God made everything and through whom we have been given life" (1 Corinthians 8:6).

One final attribute we have in common is one faith. This is a point that must be explained rather carefully. As we all know, there are many theological differences among believers. For example, there are many points of contention about the smaller matters of practice in worship. Doctrinal controversies and disagreements are all around us. So how is it that we say we have one faith? It is true because the Spirit is the One who shapes our faith. We may make many mistakes and take many wrong turns, which leads to disunity. But the genuine faith that is molded by the Holy Spirit will lead us together in unity and agreement if we will only follow Him.

There is one faith, though many misapplications of it. The Holy Spirit will always lead truly surrendered believers to the essentials. He will convict us of the reality of one crucified, resurrected, and living Christ who will return. He will always lead us to trust His Word and to devote ourselves to prayer. These are givens, and any variation from them is a sign of the Spirit's absence. There is one faith as promoted by the Spirit, and that faith can only unify us because it is the same for all of us.

As believers, we are all one body, and share one hope, one Lord, one faith, and one baptism of the Holy Spirit. And we have the same glorious heavenly Father, for we have been adopted into His spiritual family. The Bible declares, "There is only one God and Father, who is over us all and in us all and living through us all" (Ephesians 4:6).

Maintaining the Unity of the Spirit

All these reasons point to our unity as believers. But we know that many believers do not experience the unity of the body of Christ. To walk together in unity requires drawing closer and closer to our brothers and sisters in the Spirit's power. As a matter of fact, this can be seen as a good leading indicator of spiritual health. When we find that strong and supportive Christian fellowship is missing from our lives, it is a good indication that we do not know the practical meaning of Holy Spirit unity. We can remedy this problem by beginning with self-examination, taking a close look at the character qualities He is constantly developing within us.

As the Spirit molds us closer to Christ's image, we will grow in the humility of Christ. It certainly does not come naturally to this selfish and prideful world. Sin grows from pride, but humility maintains a proper and accurate perception of who we are in God's great scheme of things. We pour ourselves out for others, just as Christ poured Himself out for us. Humility enhances unity; pride creates division.

We must be gentle. We must be patient. Above all, love is absolutely essential to unity among us. True love, the kind discussed in 1 Corinthians 13, is available only through the Holy Spirit. This is why, throughout my years of ministry, I have so frequently spoken and written on the subject of how to love others by faith through the enabling of the Holy Spirit. We could never achieve supernatural, sacrificial love without allowing Him to love us and to love others through us. When we invite God to love people through us, miracles can and will happen.

As you can see, we must cultivate the attributes of Christ if we are interested in building unity. If we spend our time working with the Holy Spirit in these areas, we will have little time for focusing on the shortcomings of others in a conflict.

Preserving the Unity of the Spirit

Building unity is only part of what is required. We must also strive to maintain the harmony we have sacrificed to attain. I can assure you that our adversary, the devil, will use all of his schemes to break up our fellowship, for he knows that Christians become truly dangerous when they come together to form the body of Christ. What can we do to protect our unity?

Understand the perspectives of others. Isn't it amazing how differently we see the world when we stop to take a second look from the other person's perspective?

115

As a new Christian numerous years ago, I was quite intolerant of many other believers. I judged them as being neither hot nor cold for the Lord. In fact, I was so critical of established believers that I determined to keep those whom I led to Christ separated from them. Why let these unexcited, spiritually empty Christians pollute the zeal of the new converts? That attitude did not last long, for God helped me to see my own arrogance and pride. I had lacked any compassion for the experiences of those who had known Christ for a great deal longer than I. The Holy Spirit helped me feel love for them rather than condemnation, and I began to try looking at life from their vantage point. I reached out for opportunities to teach these older believers about the person and ministry of the Holy Spirit. Many of them were revived and became fruitful witnesses for Christ. I believe we both learned more about God from these experiences.

A little humility should help us "keep the main thing the main thing." In the New Testament, the unity of believers is a main emphasis. In disputes over minor matters of faith, we tend to put all our focus on who is in the right and who is in the wrong. The precise answer may typically be less important than we think. From the Spirit's perspective, what is *always* tremendously important is how well we love and support each other.

Throughout the New Testament, unity is lifted up as a supreme goal of the body of Christ. It is a terrible tragedy when we allow petty disagreements to corrupt that unity. The answer is to focus on the great central doctrines that unite us instead of the marginal ones that divide us. We can simply agree to disagree in areas where the Bible does not speak decisively.

We should follow the wisdom of this passage in dealing with disputes:

> Accept Christians who are weak in faith, and don't argue with them about what they think is right or wrong...Who are you to condemn God's servants? They are responsible to the Lord, so let Him tell them whether they are right or wrong. The Lord's power will help them do as they should (Romans 14:1,4).

Understanding the perspectives of others is a kind of "preventive maintenance" to help us avoid damaging conflicts.

Nurture a spirit of forgiveness, not bitterness. The world is filled with people who desperately need to be forgiven—and even more who need to forgive. Bitterness is that terrible weed that springs up in the soul and eventually chokes out all that is pure within us. It obscures our vision and perspective. It dominates our thoughts. It becomes a looming obstacle that cuts us off from perfect fellowship with God. Bitterness often begins over the smallest, most trivial slight—maybe even an imagined one. If unchecked, the root of bitterness will grow by feeding upon itself.

The devil can use bitterness more powerfully than nearly any other emotion. Eventually it becomes a cancer that will consume the spirit. Only one medicine can arrest that cancer's growth and remove it forever: forgiveness. We have another word for it in our faith, and that word is grace. The grace of God made it possible for us to be forgiven of the ultimate sin of rebellion against Him. And if He could forgive us such a great debt, there is no sin committed by another person that we are not able to forgive.

The world is filled with people who desperately need to be forgiven—and even more who need to forgive.

Jesus taught us to pray, "Forgive us our sins—just as we forgive those who have sinned against us" (Luke 11:4). The Holy Spirit wants to give us the power for that kind of forgiveness.

Initiate the building of bridges between factions. What will you do in your relationships with others? Two people can choose how to function together. They can fight a duel or sing a duet. There can be words of anger or sounds of music sweet to the ears of God. The same term used in music to mean a pleasing blend of notes can also be used to describe a reconciled relationship. That word is *harmony*, which the Bible encourages us to have as our goal: "So then, let us aim for harmony in the church and try to build each other up" (Romans 14:19).

I think we can all agree that there are enough walls in this world. My heart has broken more than once at the sight of terrible, unresolved conflicts within the body of Christ. Why is it that we find it impossible to work out our differences, all the while claiming to be guided by the Holy Spirit who craves unity and reconciliation? We need to knock down a few walls and set bridges in their place. What a refreshing experience when we are able to witness two antagonistic parties coming back together: separated spouses, schismatic church factions, bitter business partners.

Is your life more distinguished by bridges of love and harmony or by barriers of conflict and discord? How can you make peace among those torn by strife? Ask the Holy Spirit to guide you.

Treat others with love. "Most important of all, continue to show deep love for each other, for love covers a multitude of sins" (1 Peter 4:8). Here is the ultimate test of your love for others. What is it that separates you from any nonbeliever? Jesus once said, "If you are kind only to your friends, how are you different from anyone else? Even pagans do that" (Matthew 5:47). But those who are able to love their enemies give evidence of a supernatural force at work in their lives. Love will turn an enemy into a brother.

Can we practice love in daily life? I believe that of all the things we do, this is the one that most arrests the attention of a watching world. The world cannot understand how a woman can forgive the thief who broke into her home; how a worker can forgive the supervisor who cheated him; how a father can forgive the son who ran away and broke his heart; how a woman and her husband can love to Christ the man who had raped her, and then upon his release from prison, invite him to live in their house for a while. The world knows that a greater force than human emotion must be at work—a force that transcends selfishness and retribution, a force that is willing to endure undeserved pain in order to serve another human being. The world has no explanation for something so remarkable that shows them that Jesus is more than a man, and Christianity is more than a religion. Where all our careful arguments and presentations fail to move someone, the reality of authentic love is utterly persuasive.

Nothing is more powerful than God's love. "And the most important piece of clothing you must wear is love. Love is what binds us all together in perfect harmony" (Colossians 3:14). Let God show love through you, in unity and harmony, and the world will come hurrying to learn more about the One who inspires such love and unity.

Yield to one another out of respect for Christ. If we can love one another, we can yield to one another. Yielding is the outward proof of inward love. Christ yielded Himself to the Father in all things. As His followers, we should yield ourselves not only to Him but also to one another, as an example of our respect for Jesus: "Submit to one another out of reverence for Christ" (Ephesians 5:21).

If I were to ask you how you felt about those in your local body of believers, I expect you would immediately tell me how you loved them. Most of us can love in principle. The hard part is loving by application. What if you had a tremendous idea for your Bible study group, and you spent hours planning it and working out the details— only to have another member submit a competing plan? You may well love that fellow member, but are you willing to yield? If you truly love your fellow believers, you will submit to them frequently for the good of the body and the will of the Lord. There can be healthy and positive discussion of alternatives, but love requires us to yield frequently. The Spirit will gently prod you on those occasions when you need to step back and put aside your pride.

Make Peace—But Not at All Costs

As we have suggested, there are times when unity will inevitably suffer. What if someone were to stand in your church or Christian group and proclaim that Jesus, Buddha, and Mohammed should now be considered as equals? What if a leader challenged the historicity of the resurrection of Jesus Christ? We must face the fact that there are some authentic issues that should be fought for, even if unity suffers. The truth is that there can be no long-term unity if heresy is embraced. The Holy Spirit will not tolerate its presence.

Believers are called to be peacemakers, but not to elevate the modern idea of "tolerance" above truth. Tolerance should never be confused with love or extended for the sake of unity. We are called to love one another and to treat each other respectfully, just as we would like to be treated. But if we tolerate immoral behavior or misguided, heretical teaching for any reason, we are no longer light and salt to those who are perishing. We must never compromise God's biblical truth.

Having firmly stated that, we must recognize that the greater number of Christian disputes do not have these central areas of doctrinal integrity at their center. They may be about anything from church carpet color to political power to personality differences. Those are the issues the Spirit will help you conquer in the name of loving Christian unity. If we allow the smaller conflicts to tear us asunder, the world will shake its head and conclude that we are no different from anyone else. But when the Holy Spirit's sacrificial, yielding love and compassion prevail, something special can be seen by everyone. Only then can we become a city set on a hill, ablaze with light. Only then can we become salt and light to an unbelieving world.

Jesus said, "Your love for one another will prove to the world that you are My disciples" (John 13:35). The Spirit's love and unity are miraculous, unique, and beyond anything the world can possibly manufacture. Ask the Holy Spirit today to make you an instrument of His divine love to promote unity in your family, church, community, and country.

In the next chapter, we will explore the Holy Spirit's protection in the midst of spiritual assaults.

Life Application

 Meditate on the Words of the Spirit. Take some time to memorize and meditate on the following verses:

- ■ "Make every effort to keep the unity of the Spirit through the bond of peace. There is one body and one Spirit—just as you were called to one hope when you were called" (Ephesians 4:3,4, NIV).

- ■ "May God, who gives this patience and encouragement, help you live in complete harmony with each other—each with the attitude of Christ Jesus toward the other" (Romans 15:5).

 Focus on the Presence of the Spirit. Contemplate the following questions:

- ■ Have you ever contributed to a division in your home or church? How can you remedy this situation?

- ■ What attitudes do you harbor—prejudice, insecurity, jealousy, a love for gossip—that get in the way of being at peace with other believers?

- ■ How does God want you to treat your fellow brothers and sisters in Christ?

 Walk in the Power of the Spirit. Jesus Christ wants His body to be unified, not divided. The Holy Spirit is His instrument to bring harmony and deep community by cleansing us, transforming us, and uniting us in divine love. Commit yourself to practicing the truths in the UNITY acrostic:

Understand the perspectives of others.

Nurture a spirit of forgiveness, not bitterness.

Initiate the building of bridges between factions.

Treat others with love.

Yield to one another out of respect for Christ.

Pray today for the various Christian groups to which you belong. Ask God to bring them together in perfect unity in the Spirit, that they would experience the same love that exists between Jesus and the Father.

Chapter 9

Our Protector from Evil

I t happens all around us: an invisible war. You are a fighter in it, and I am, too. This war is the conflict that we as Christians call spiritual warfare.

Make no mistake: this is authentic war with authentic, invisible enemies. The Word of God tells us, "For we are not fighting against people made of flesh and blood, but against the evil rulers and authorities of the unseen world, against those mighty powers of darkness who rule this world, and against wicked spirits in the heavenly realms" (Ephesians 6:12).

Satan entices the mind, titillates the senses, and uses our areas of weakness to provoke sin and ruin the purity of our fellowship. It is no wonder that Jesus taught His disciples to pray, "Don't let us yield to temptation, but deliver us from the evil one" (Matthew 6:13).

But if the enemy is a powerful creature rather than one of flesh and blood, and if he is infinitely more intelligent than we are, and if he has had all of human history to perfect his deceit and trickery, how can we possibly hope to do battle with him—let alone win?

Equipped for Battle

The Bible reveals that we have spiritual weaponry for fighting spiritual battles: "Put on all of God's armor so that you will be able to stand firm against all strategies and tricks of the Devil" (Ephesians 6:11). Paul made use of the Roman military terminology of his day to help us understand that indeed, life is a spiritual battle; we cannot afford to go out unprepared.

Faith, salvation, truth, the Word—we seldom think of these as armor, but this is precisely what they are. If believers are going to stop surrendering to the flesh, the world, and the devil, we must learn to fight spiritually. We must put on all the armor of the spiritual warrior. Let us examine them one by one.

The Word of God commands believers to put on "the sturdy belt of truth" (Ephesians 6:14). Before a Roman soldier went into battle, he rolled up his long robe waist high and then secured it with a sash or girdle. If he did not, his movements would be hindered. We, too, are to gird ourselves with truth—God's Word. We need to think biblically so that faulty, misguided ideas will not get in the way of our living for our Lord (Philippians 4:8).

Most of us know where our weak spots are. Be assured that Satan will choose those precise points as his targets.

We also wear the "body armor of God's righteousness" (Ephesians 6:14). The armor of Paul's time was a breastplate covering the chest and abdomen which protected the wearer from being wounded by his enemy's sword. Our enemy loves to defeat us by reminding us of our unworthiness. But if we have confessed our sin to God, we are covered with Christ's righteousness. The devil fires his flaming darts of deadly accusation, but the armor of the righteousness of Christ completely covers us.

"For shoes, put on the peace that comes from the Good News, so that you will be fully prepared" (Ephesians 6:15). No good soldier would wear an ordinary shoe or sandal into battle. Roman soldiers wore boots with embedded nails that functioned like today's cleats. When marching through mud, they would not slip. The Good News of the gospel provides solid spiritual footing for each of us.

The next piece of armor we are to take up is "faith as your shield to stop the fiery arrows aimed at you by Satan" (Ephesians 6:16). The clever enemies of Rome often dipped their arrows in hot tar, set them afire, then fired them on their deadly journeys. The Romans, of course, could take shelter behind their shields, which were often as tall as wooden doors. Strong faith in Christ is our hiding place and shelter when it seems the world is shooting flaming arrows at us from every direction.

Then you should "put on salvation as your helmet" (Ephesians 6:17). Any good soldier needs to keep a level head—literally! In the heat of combat, the helmet was essential for the battlefield, particularly when facing the broad sword. The breastplate and shield might protect a soldier from nearly all the flaming darts, but his head would still be exposed from above. Salvation protects the mind. Our souls are safe, and we can fight victoriously on the battlefield through the power of the Holy Spirit.

Finally, we wield as our only weapon "the sword of the Spirit, which is the word of God" (Ephesians 6:17). The Roman soldiers used long, heavy broad swords and small, swift daggers. The larger sword was brought down on the head of a foe; the smaller dagger was deadly when driven through an enemy's armor toward a vulnerable spot. The Word of God is like the dagger—quick, powerful, and sharp. The Scriptures are so penetrating that they can defeat any adversary, immediately plunging through a weak spot to the heart of the matter. Think of how Jesus used the Scriptures to defeat the devil's temptations in the desert. In the greatest of our trials, the Word of God pierces the darkness, pointing accurately to truth when confusion is all around us. Read God's Word every day. Study it, memorize it, and apply its truths to your daily living.

Exposing the Father of Lies

It is amazing to consider the web of lies and deceit that surrounds us at all times. A spider's webbing is so thin that it is nearly invisible, but the lies of the devil are even more elusive. We could be ensnared at any time if not for the Spirit, who exposes the Great Deceiver. Satan prefers to work not in the open but through deception and trickery, with a skill and cunning he has learned through centuries of experience.

The devil has a personal strategy for each individual believer. Most of us know where our weak spots are. Be assured that he will choose those precise points as his targets. If your marriage is not strong, that is the place where he will surely try to break through your lines of defense and harm you spiritually. If you struggle with honesty in business, he will throw temptation after temptation at you in this area.

I remember a young man I met during my days in seminary. He had come home from the mission field filled with defeat. I listened carefully as he described his frustration and despair. It was clear that he was living in the energy of the flesh, which amounts to going onto the battlefield day after day without armor. I explained this to the young man and told him he desperately needed to be filled with the Spirit.

His response was an angry one. Had he not been serving on the mission field for years? Had he not given of himself sacrificially to reach people for Christ? He stormed out of my office.

After deeper consideration, he called me and asked for a second meeting where we continued our discussion of the Holy Spirit. A few days later I heard from the young man by mail. He had asked God to confirm to him whether my words were true, and the Spirit acknowledged within him that indeed they were true. My friend invited the Holy Spirit to fill him, and he shared with me the joy and excitement of his new discovery.

Jesus said, "When the Spirit of truth comes, He will guide you into all truth" (John 16:13). Just as the Spirit overcame the deception that this young man was doing all the right things, He will point you to all the truth you need. We simply need to ask Him to do so, as this believer did.

The World, the Flesh, and the Devil

For many centuries, Christian scholars have spoken of a three-pronged attack that believers must face when encountering temptation. The attacks are from the world, the flesh, and the devil. They are interrelated, and they overlap—but each of these three should be considered individually.

First, we face temptations of a worldly variety. In the Bible, "the world" is a term that refers to the ordered, arranged system of physical reality that is under Satan's control. The devil himself is referred to as "the prince of this world" (John 12:31). The world, biblically speaking, includes the people who follow his deceptions as well as their false beliefs. We are "worldly," then, when we get out of step with the Spirit and fall in line with Satan's crooked path—when we come under the influences of worldly people, values, or convictions.

Worldliness can be very subtle. Many Christians fall under the spell of materialism, for example. But there are many other forms of worldliness. To combat the lure of this world, we should reflect on the following passage:

> Stop loving this evil world and all that it offers you, for when you love the world, you show that you do not have the love of the Father in you. For the world offers only the lust for physical pleasure, the lust for everything we see, and pride in our possessions. These are not from the Father. They are from this evil world. And this world is fading away, along with everything it craves. But if you do the will of God, you will live forever (1 John 2:15–17).

In dealing with the temptation of worldliness, you still must face the lure of the flesh. What is the biblical meaning of this term? The flesh is the earthly part of man with its lusts and desires. The Bible teaches us that living according to the flesh is a sure road to death. The way of the flesh includes not only hunger, lust, and other appetites, but also impulses such as anger and greed. When we ignore the guidance of the Spirit, we are certain to live in the flesh and will make ourselves as miserable as the rest of the world.

Praise God that His Spirit helps us crucify the flesh. If you are a slave to impulsive eating, the Spirit will help you place that fleshly sin on the cross, where Christ has already died to keep it from having power over you. If you struggle to control your thoughts from wandering toward sexual impurity, the Spirit will put that tendency to death. "Our old sinful selves were crucified with Christ so that sin might lose its power in our lives. We are no longer slaves to sin . . . So you should consider yourselves dead to sin and able to live for the glory of God through Christ Jesus" (Romans 6:6,11). Much of our spiritual growth and maturity comes through the painful sacrifice of cooperating with the Spirit, moment by moment and day by day.

The third attack of sin and temptation is that of the devil himself. He is ultimately behind all temptation; he is the unseen enemy. But there are times when he steps forward to challenge us personally. This

127

is why the Bible admonishes us, "Be careful! Watch out for attacks from the Devil, your great enemy. He prowls around like a roaring lion, looking for some victim to devour" (1 Peter 5:8). But what will happen when we stand tall against the devil himself? How astonished will the world be to see us stand firm under the attack of the worst temptations he has to offer? You cannot face the lion from hell unless you have the strength of the Lion of Judah. You must fight the hellfire of Satan with the holy fire of the Spirit. He will protect you through the armor of spiritual warfare. He will give you shelter behind the shield of faith and help you strike back, powerfully using the sword of the Spirit, the Word of God.

We can triumph over Satan in the coliseum of life only because the Victor Himself, Jesus Christ, lives within us through His Spirit.

Preparing for Battle

There are several things we can do to prepare for battle and assure victory over temptation. First, *we must claim God's promises for victory over temptation.* The Scriptures offer us powerful ammunition for standing firm in the times we are tempted the most. There are several liberating promises in the following passage alone:

> No temptation has overtaken you but such as is common to man; and God is faithful, who will not allow you to be tempted beyond what you are able, but with the temptation will provide the way of escape also, that you will be able to endure it (1 Corinthians 10:13, NASB).

We feel isolated and alone when we struggle on the verge of disobedience. We think that no one can help, no one can understand what we are experiencing. But the Bible promises us that other people also face such temptations every day, and that God never fails to provide self-control to His children when they seek His help. Not only that, but the temptation will never be sizeable enough that we will have no chance of victory over it. We are promised that He will not allow a temptation that we cannot overcome with His help, and He always offers an escape route. This is wonderful news! Simply by claiming the promises in 1 Corinthians 10, as I have done on thousands of occasions, we are well on the road to victory.

Second, *in preparing to face temptation, we must occupy our minds with thoughts that are pleasing to God.* The Bible urges us, "Don't copy the behavior and customs of this world, but let God transform you into a new person by changing the way you think. Then you will know what God wants you to do, and you will know how good and pleasing and perfect His will really is" (Romans 12:2).

Third, when tempted, *we should always unite with other believers in prayer.* Call a "war council" prayer meeting of Christians you really trust, and trust them with the trials you are facing. As they pray daily for you, you will feel bolstered by new power and resolve such as you have never experienced. The Bible assures us, "The earnest prayer of a righteous person has great power and wonderful results" (James 5:16).

God will honor you for your humility in seeking the prayerful support of your fellow Christians. He will bless not only your life but the lives of those who come to your aid. It is also true that we are far less likely to commit a sin when our friends and family are holding us accountable.

In the Heat of Conflict

You have done your "preventive maintenance work" and fortified yourself spiritually. But still temptation comes; we will continue to face it, because we are human. What can we do in the line of fire? For one thing, we can resist Satan and his schemes.

Does that sound too simplistic? There is nothing new or exciting about the idea that the answer to temptation is to resist it. The world would have us believe resistance is impossible, but we are not as weak as the modern world wants to tell us we are. From the magazines and movies of our time, one would think no married person could resist the lure of adultery, that everyone must eventually give in and cheat in business and on their taxes. But as we daily offer our bodies as living sacrifices to our wonderful Lord, the ideas of corruption and disobedience should become more and more repugnant to us. We should become more committed in our resolve to stand firm, to resist the temptation and send the devil on his way.

The command of the Bible is beautifully simple and direct as well: "Submit yourselves, then, to God. Resist the devil, and he will flee from you" (James 4:7, NIV). This is simple cause and effect: resist the temptation, and it will go away and leave you in peace for now. Keep resisting it whenever it returns, and you will gain strength. Keep giving in, and you are headed down a slippery slope to spiritual self-destruction. The key comes at the beginning of that passage. When we submit ourselves to God, we have placed Him before our own desires and appetites. We will seek to please Him in all things.

Submission strengthens our resolve and focuses our perspective. When the temptation comes, therefore, we see it in the light of our relationship with Him. Then we can resist and watch the devil as he scurries away. Is that not a great moment of victory?

When we submit ourselves to God, we have placed Him before our own desires and appetites.

What is your most troublesome temptation? Whatever it might be, I have confidence that you can stand firm against it. But never attempt to do so without the proper weapon in your hand. You should always arm yourself with the sword of the Spirit. I can tell you that our greatest weapon in the face of inner conflict is the Word of God wielded with the power of the Spirit of God.

God's Word is the objective, eternal truth for all believers. God's Spirit, on the other hand, is His presence in our individual lives. If we had the Bible alone, the truth would seem cold and impersonal; if we had only the Holy Spirit, the truth would be subjectively misapplied based on our personal biases. But when we put the objective Word in the hands of the Spirit who knows us individually and intimately, there is no crisis we cannot face. There is no temptation too large. I cannot explain this concept with any greater clarity than to quote what the Word says about itself:

> The word of God is full of living power. It is sharper than the sharpest knife, cutting deep into our innermost thoughts and desires. It exposes us for what we really are. Nothing in all creation can hide from Him. Everything is naked and exposed before His

eyes. This is the God to whom we must explain all that we have done (Hebrews 4:12,13).

So there you stand, resisting temptation on the foundation of the Word of God, applied by the Spirit of God. Simply realizing that His strength is on your side will encourage you. Victory is assured. And as you face the future, how could you not be stronger and wiser in the face of future temptation?

Preparing for the Next Battle

As we look to the devil's next attack, we can be prepared by guarding our affections. We cannot serve the world and our Lord at the same time. Only one will win out. We must make a choice—sometimes many times in a day—between yielding to our old nature and the world's ways, and living by the Spirit and God's ways.

Have you let bad habits or poor choices get a grip on your affections? If those things have a hold on you, the devil's work is much easier. The key to guarding your affections and keeping them free of those entanglements is to abide in Christ through the Holy Spirit. Jesus tells us in the Gospel of John, "I am the vine; you are the branches. If a man remains in Me and I in him, he will bear much fruit; apart from Me you can do nothing" (John 15:5, NIV). As you abide in Him, through prayer, reflection, and the Word, He will be actively performing a great work in you. When you turn your eyes upon Jesus, as the old hymn says, "the things of earth will grow strangely dim, in the light of His glory and grace." What is happening? You are being remade into the image of Christ. As you let the Spirit do His work, you will behave and feel a bit more like Christ today than you did yesterday.

As that happens, your loving affection for Him will grow deeper and deeper. You will see that only He can truly satisfy. And when the devil comes along with cheap, empty substitutes for God's joy and fulfillment, you will see those things for what they are—and the devil's task will be much more difficult. Guard your affections and give God your greatest love, your greatest time, your greatest commitment. Never give the devil a foothold.

Finally, as you face the future and its trials, expect God to prevail—and thank Him for every victory. In the presence of sustained and overwhelming opposition, we need to remember what God has done in the past, where He is at work right now, and what He has promised for a wonderful future. We must stop behaving as if we were a defeated enemy—we know that Christ will have the final victory; that He is greater than he who is in the world; that there is no temptation greater than His power in us; and that daily victory through the enabling of the Holy Spirit is ours for the asking. We should have the greatest confidence in passing every test with flying colors.

As our faith and confidence grow in that light, we begin to see ourselves differently. The Bible says that "we are more than conquerors through Him who loved us" (Romans 8:37, NIV). When we face temptation, we should never feel isolated, weak, or helpless. Whatever the devil may try to tell you, you are in fact a conqueror—a champion! For now, you are running the race with all the concentration and endurance that effort requires. But in the end, you are promised that every ounce of spiritual fortitude will be made worthwhile. The Bible speaks of the victor's crown that awaits you: "God blesses the people who patiently endure testing. Afterward they will receive the crown of life that God has promised to those who love Him" (James 1:12).

That, my friend, is a crown worth waiting for. Imagine arriving home after a hard day in which you skipped lunch. You rummage around in the kitchen and find a candy bar. Just as you lift it toward your mouth, your spouse walks into the kitchen and says, "Hey, that thing will spoil your appetite—I was going to take you to the finest restaurant in town!" I believe you would put the cheap candy bar away quickly. Why let it take the edge off a far greater, far more delicious feast that lies in store for you?

There is no temptation, no matter how powerful, that would not pale in the light of the reward that awaits you and me in heaven. I want to run the race and be counted worthy of that crown. I want to avoid those entanglements that could trip me up and keep me from running at full speed. I have a goal that is greater than anything the world can offer, and I intend to keep letting the Spirit give me power, wisdom, and victory in the face of the most alluring temptations this dark world can offer. I leave you with this challenge from the Old Testament:

> "Take your positions; then stand still and watch the LORD's victory. He is with you, O people of Judah and Jerusalem. Do not be afraid or discouraged. Go out there tomorrow, for the LORD is with you!" (2 Chronicles 20:17).

In the next chapter we will look at spiritual gifts and how they help us fulfill God's plan for us.

Life Application

 Meditate on the Words of the Spirit. Memorize and meditate on the following verses from this chapter:

- "The Spirit who lives in you is greater than the spirit who lives in the world" (1 John 4:4).

- "Submit yourselves, then, to God. Resist the devil, and he will flee from you" (James 4:7, NIV).

 Focus on the Presence of the Spirit. Prayerfully answer these questions about your life:

- Do you believe Satan actively wants to discourage you and stunt your growth in the Lord? Have you recognized his tactics in the past? Was he successful?

- What areas of your life are challenged by the world, the flesh, and the devil?

- How can you guard against these attacks?

 Walk in the Power of the Spirit. The Holy Spirit living in you is more powerful than any temptation. He longs to protect you and embolden you toward victory. As a warrior trains for battle, prepare yourself for attack by practicing the steps found in the COURAGE acrostic:

Claim God's promises for victory over temptation.

Occupy your mind with thoughts that are pleasing to God.

Unite with other believers in prayer.

Resist Satan and his schemes.

Arm yourself with the sword of the Spirit.

Guard your affections.

Expect God to prevail and thank Him for every victory.

Ask God today to point out the weak spots where the devil is getting a foothold in your life. Then trust the Spirit to give you victory in shutting out any opportunity for disobedience.

Chapter 10

Our Source for Service

Anyone would agree that Ernest Hemingway had special gifts. He wrote memorable, best-selling novels such as *The Sun Also Rises*, *A Farewell to Arms*, and *For Whom the Bell Tolls*. He won both a Pulitzer and a Nobel Prize, yet he found time for all kinds of adventures in his globe-trotting life. He fought in a world war, flew planes, fished in deep-sea waters, fought bulls, and generally served as the very icon of the "macho" American adventurer. His rugged image, his work, and his ideas were known all over the world—and some have claimed that his writing style was the most influential of the century.

Yet in 1961, he removed himself from a tortured existence by taking his own life. How could this be? Why would someone with such a lust for life, and so many gifts to offer the world, commit suicide?

Meanwhile, unannounced in the headlines, there are countless "little" people across the world—living quiet lives, having never fought a bull, wrestled a championship marlin, or written a classic novel. These folks find fulfillment, excitement, and sheer joy just the same. They find their significance not through publicity, power, and personal gifts, but through godly power and spiritual gifts. They have found something that shines so brightly it leaves money and fame in the shadows. What they have found makes their life count not for a season but for eternity. And as a result, they have the kind of wonderful peace and heartfelt joy that Ernest Hemingway and so many others were never able to grasp.

An author may write a masterpiece if he is extremely fortunate and productive with his craft. It may remain in print for a few decades or, very rarely, for a few centuries. But the Bible claims that you are a masterpiece of heavenly art: "For we are God's masterpiece," Paul wrote. "He has created us anew in Christ Jesus, so that we can do the good things He planned for us long ago" (Ephesians 2:10). God created you as a thing of beauty to last for all eternity. Like all great art, you bear the stamp and style of the Artist who produced you.

Best of all, you are an *active* work of art. You are a masterpiece created with a function: to do "good things" that He laid out for you even before you were born. Think of a loving human father who is waiting for his infant son to be born. He buys a baseball glove and places it in the closet, eager for his child to reach the age when he can discover the joy of breaking in that glove and playing catch with Dad. The father dreams of that moment. This is the joy God feels about your gifts. This is how He awaits your discovery of the work He has set aside for you.

Gifts are never meant to be used in isolation. God gives them to you for edifying the body of Christ.

You are a masterpiece even now, whether you know it or not. But the best is yet to come. When you discover what He created you to do, and you begin to fulfill that bright destiny, your joy will be exceeded only by the joy of your Creator who has planned it all along. In this chapter we will talk about those thrilling tasks and gifts that await you.

The Life of the Body

Have you ever thought about how God sees your life? He sees past, present, and future as if they were all one, for He does not dwell within time as we do. Our minutes, days, and years are a created structure within His eternity. From His place in eternity, He looks upon your life as a whole unit. He knows the gifts He designed for you, and He knows the tasks that need to be fulfilled. He carefully crafted your gifts and your personality to fill those needs, and He placed you in just the right position to be confronted by those needs one day. All that remains is for you to find the gift, discover the need, and do what God designed you to do.

On the day when the Holy Spirit entered your life at salvation, those gifts began to percolate, even if you were unaware of them. The Spirit is the one who activates your gifts and begins to mold them toward service. He is the one who lightly nudges you and whispers in your ear when you come to the moment of exercising them—like taking out that baseball glove for the first time.

It is also the Spirit who works powerfully through your gifts, in a way that astounds you. "Aha!" you'll gasp. "This is the very thing I was meant to do. In this, I can fulfill my potential for God, and it feels good." You have discovered something precious and irreplaceable: dynamic purpose. God has a wonderful plan for your life, and you have taken the first steps toward discovering what it is.

One of the most wonderful traits of spiritual gifts is the way they bond you with other believers. Gifts are never meant to be used in isolation. God gives them to you for edifying the body of Christ. Unless you use your gifts, something will be missing in your local Christian fellowship. People will lack something of value. And if others fail to use their gifts, you will lack something as well.

It is no coincidence that the Bible calls the church the "body of Christ." He is the head, and each of us is a body part. "Just as our bodies have many parts and each part has a special function, so it is with Christ's body. We are all parts of His one body, and each of us has different work to do. And since we are all one body in Christ, we belong to each other, and each of us needs all the others" (Romans 12:4,5). Jesus left the world forty days after His resurrection, but in a miraculous manner, He created a way to continue being present and active in it, right up to this day. His body lives and walks and serves through the accumulation of believers indwelt by the Spirit who are using their gifts.

Jesus created His church to be a community that works with the same beautiful complexity as the parts of a human body. The human body is God's physical masterpiece, and the church is His spiritual one. In both cases, a wound to one part means pain for the whole body. A broken finger means that a physical body will feel the ache and be hampered in all that it tries to do. A suffering church member means that the body of Christ will experience pain and malfunction. We were never intended to be independent agents as believers. We need each other vitally, and we cannot fully experience the Christian life without the give and take of functioning in the body.

Paul explains our interdependence this way: "Suppose the whole body were an eye—then how would you hear? Or if your whole body were just one big ear, how could you smell anything?" (1 Corinthians 12:17). It is a great mistake to suppose that all Christians should be carbon copies of one another, for diversity is what allows us to accomplish such a wide array of tasks in building God's kingdom. Instead of allowing our differences to divide us, we should be realizing that they are the very distinctions that make us special. Diversity shows the genius of God's design. He made us with unique gifts, varying perspectives, and distinct personalities so we could thrive as a healthy body and complete the tasks He has for us here on earth. Each of us is a vital part of the body of Christ.

Equipped to Fulfill God's Plan

The glue that holds the body of Christ together, of course, is the Holy Spirit. Without the Spirit we would have no hope of ever finding unity. It is the same Spirit who allows one to be a helper and another a teacher, one to be an administrator and another an encourager. When we are in tune with Him, we see the big picture; we recognize the marvelous way we complement each other. The Spirit binds us together in love and bestows upon us unique gifts to accomplish, step by step, the plan Christ has for His church.

The topic of gifts is an intriguing and controversial one. The biblical word for gifts is *charisma*, which means "gifts of grace." The Bible teaches that they are given to us as tools of individual service, provided so that we may build up the body of Christ and fulfill God's plan for the church and the world. As the Word explains, "God has given each of us the ability to do certain things well" (Romans 12:6).

The Holy Spirit provides every single believer with at least one spiritual gift: "It is the same and only Holy Spirit who distributes these gifts. He alone decides which gift each person should have" (1 Corinthians 12:11). You may have one gift or you may have several. No matter how insignificant a member of the body may seem, the Bible promises that this person is an integral part of the body of Christ with special spiritual abilities. This concept should certainly affect the way we treat one another within the church—and it should also affect the way you think of yourself as a member of the body.

Perhaps your life is like Ira Yates' sheep ranch. During the Great Depression in the 1930s, his ranch offered insufficient financial support for his family. He struggled to pay off the mortgage and was in danger of losing his land to the bank. His family began living on a government subsidy. Then a seismographic crew from an oil company came to visit and asked permission to drill a test well on Yates' land. At 1,115 feet, the drillers struck oil. The first well came in at 80,000 barrels a day. On today's market, that would be about 2.5 million dollars a day. Many more wells were drilled and the amazing success continued; some of them were twice as productive as the first. Yates, the one-time sheep-rancher, had been sitting on a financial empire without knowing it. He was a multi-millionaire who had been living in poverty.

You may look at your life as a barren property, yet the Bible promises that there are riches buried within. You are endowed with gifts that make you capable of doing what no one else could do in the same way. It is crucially important that you find and use your gifts; otherwise, neither you nor the local body of Christ will be able to fulfill the wonderful plan God has for you. The moment you identify a gift and begin turning it toward service, wonderful things will happen. "God has given gifts to each of you from His great variety of spiritual gifts. Manage them well so that God's generosity can flow through you" (1 Peter 4:10).

And what are these gifts? A number of them are mentioned in the New Testament:

- Apostleship (1 Corinthians 12:28; Ephesians 4:11)
- Prophecy (1 Corinthians 12:10; Romans 12:6; Ephesians 4:11)
- Teaching (1 Corinthians 12:28,29; Romans 12:7)

- Helping/serving (1 Corinthians 12:28; Romans 12:7)
- Showing mercy/kindness (Romans 12:8)
- Evangelism (Ephesians 4:11)
- Pastor/teacher (Ephesians 4:11)
- Leadership (Romans 12:8)
- Administration (1 Corinthians 12:28)
- Giving (Romans 12:8)
- Special faith (1 Corinthians 12:9)
- Exhortation/Encouragement (Romans 12:8)
- Wisdom (1 Corinthians 12:8)
- Knowledge (1 Corinthians 12:8)
- Discerning of spirits (1 Corinthians 12:10)
- Working of miracles (1 Corinthians 12:10)
- Healing (1 Corinthians 12:9)
- Speaking in tongues (1 Corinthians 12:10)
- Interpreting tongues (1 Corinthians 12:10)

Please know that this list is not exhaustive—there could be others that are unnamed. God has many purposes and His Spirit will enable you to fulfill whatever task He needs you to do at the time. But these are the gifts listed in the Bible, and they are the ones traditionally identified and observed among active believers. (Each of these gifts is explained in Appendix A.) At least one of these should be present in your life.

For Glory and for Growth

The gifts of the Spirit glorify Christ. As that occurs, the church will grow in size and strength. It is important to remember that in no way should our gifts puff us up with pride or fill us with any delusions of grandeur. True spiritual gifts never point to our glory but only to the magnificence of Christ. As you observe a gifted teacher or evangelist, you will observe how this question is answered: To what extent do this person's gifts glorify Christ? To what extent do they magnify this person's ego?

As we observe a gifted administrator, for example, it will become clear whether this person uses his or her gift to fulfill the purposes of Christ or to solidify personal power. The visible gifts, such as these, tend to be the ones in danger of being misused—and the Spirit will discipline believers who misappropriate the precious gifts they have been given for their own benefits.

The Bible states the case this way: "Are you called to be a speaker? Then speak as though God Himself were speaking through you. Are you called to help others? Do it with all the strength and energy that God supplies. Then God will be given glory in everything through Jesus Christ. All glory and power belong to Him forever and ever" (1 Peter 4:11). Gifts are focused fully and constantly upon the glory of God, plain and simple. When any controversy arises concerning them, this is an important truth to keep in mind. How is the name of Christ exalted and glorified? If Christ is not the center of focus, spiritual gifts are not being properly used.

As each member of the body of Christ exercises his or her gifts, we are continuing Christ's work on earth.

As each member of the body of Christ exercises his or her gifts, we are continuing Christ's work on earth. Theologian and author J. I. Packer explains in his book *Keep in Step with the Spirit,* "Our exercise of spiritual gifts is nothing more nor less than Christ himself ministering through his body to his body, to the Father, and to all mankind. From heaven Christ uses Christians as his mouth, his hands, his feet, even his smile; it is through us, his people, that he speaks and acts, meets, loves, and saves here and now in this world."[1]

Two thousand years ago, Jesus lived upon the earth and ministered to people. After He departed for heaven to sit at the right hand of the Father, He appointed His Spirit to carry on His work through us—not in a vague, symbolic sense but in a true, supernatural one. He once delivered His teachings in Israel; He now delivers them across the world through us. He once traveled among all the towns and provinces there; He now travels to every inhabited continent and nation through us. He once performed miracles to the people of His time; He now performs them in our time through us. He once healed people, loved people, encouraged people, and showed them a new way to live. All of those things are happening today through you and me, manifesting our gifts as His living body. We are His hands, His feet, His presence in the world. And we glorify Him.

As Christ is exalted through our gifts, the church continues to be blessed and enlarged. "A spiritual gift is given to each of us as a means of helping the entire church" (1 Corinthians 12:7). Our gifts are for the good of the whole, as if we were the individual cells in the human body. That body remains healthy when each cell performs its appointed task. If the cells rebelled and stopped working for the good of the entire human body, we would have what is known medically as cancer. A healthy church needs healthy, selfless members using their gifts to glorify Christ and strengthen His body through the good of the fellowship. When the church breaks into factions and power struggles, the "cells" have become cancerous.

Imagine also a human body in which a few of the cells were expected to perform all the body's functions. I think you will agree that the health prognosis for this individual would not be good. We see that spiritually when a church expects its pastor and staff to do all the ministry. We tend to use a "professional" paradigm for the church, expressing that we pay these men to do the work for us. But the Bible teaches that every member is to serve; everyone has been given gifts to use, and each one is necessary.

Putting Your Gifts to Work

God wants His children to experience the contentment and joy that come from serving Him in the power of the Holy Spirit. How can you begin today to put your gifts to work for the good of the body of Christ?

First, identify your gifts through the confirmation of others as you serve. Some ministries have developed simple written tests to help you think about your aptitudes and tendencies, and thus discover what your gifts might be. But the best way for you to learn what the Spirit has equipped you to do is through service. Minister in a wide variety of opportunities and discover where you are the most effective, where you derive the greatest sense of satisfaction, where Christ is most glorified and your fellow members are most strengthened. I believe that if you set about doing this in your church, you will soon begin to learn about your gifts.

But the important thing is to be active in service. As the apostle Paul admonished his "son" in the faith, Timothy, "Do not neglect the spiritual gift you received" (1 Timothy 4:14).

Second, give of your gifts in love through the power of the Holy Spirit. "Pursue love, yet desire earnestly spiritual gifts" (1 Corinthians 14:1, NASB). Never let your focus move to yourself, but keep it on serving Christ and His body. As always, the key to doing that is found in the most wonderful of all words, *love*. If you begin to regard others as more important than yourself and look to their benefit, you will find yourself using your gifts—almost without realizing it.

Remember the beautiful poetry of 1 Corinthians 13, where Paul writes:

> If I had the gift of being able to speak in other languages without learning them, and could speak in every language there is in all of heaven and earth, but didn't love others, I would only be making noise. If I had the gift of prophecy and knew all about what is going to happen in the future, knew everything about everything, but didn't love others, what good would it do? Even if I had the gift of faith so that I could speak to a mountain and make it move, I would still be worth nothing at all without love. If I gave everything I have to poor people, and if I were burned alive for preaching the Gospel but didn't love others, it would be of no value whatever" (1 Corinthians 13:1–3, TLB).

What more can be said? No matter what you accomplish, no matter how hard you work, your gifts will amount to nothing without love. Used in the service of love for Christ and His church, however, they will make an eternal impact.

As you begin using and developing your gifts, you will be fulfilling God's purpose for your life. Again, Paul wrote to Timothy, "Fan into flames the spiritual gift God gave you when I laid my hands on you" (2 Timothy 1:6).

The symbol of fire and flame is often used in relation to the Holy Spirit. Paul's word picture here is one of a spark starting a great, spreading fire of God's power. Imagine that you have the gift of helps. Your enthusiastic and Spirit-led use of that gift will be infectious. As you begin developing a whole program of assisting needy people, for example, other people with that same gift will emerge from all around you. They will be inspired to follow your example. One gift will lead to another. This will occur as you develop your gifts through following the Holy Spirit, giving of your time, and working as hard as you can to serve through your spiritual gifts. Each year you should attempt to be a little better and a little more comprehensive in the ministry of your spiritual gifts.

Your Gifts in Perspective

Our final two directives relate to putting your spiritual gifts into greater perspective within your life and the life of your local fellowship.

First, think rightly about yourself and your gifts. Paul wrote to the Christians in Rome, "As God's messenger, I give each of you this warning: Be honest in your estimate of yourselves, measuring your value by how much faith God has given you" (Romans 12:3). Humility is not necessarily lowering one's estimate of oneself, but being more accurate in that assessment. On the one hand, you are irreplaceable and eternally significant in your place in the body of Christ. The church will never be what God intends it to be unless you are there exercising your gifts. On the other hand, this is no occasion for pride; it is the Spirit who has the power, the Spirit who provides the ability, and the Spirit who does the work through you. Balance your view of self with a thorough understanding of these points.

Avoid the misconception that there is some kind of hierarchy of gifts. There is a long-standing myth that "visible" gifts such as teacher or pastor are more important or glamorous. People with these gifts are at the center of attention. Those with gifts such as giving, on the other hand, can be nearly invisible. These gifts may be practiced quietly,

146

sometimes anonymously. But in truth, the proper use of gifts means that none are glamorous at all—they all magnify Christ, and the encourager of one hurting soul is just as precious to God as the teacher of five thousand. We are to decrease that He may increase.

Also, trying to implement someone else's gift will leave you frustrated and miserable. Your greatest joy, satisfaction, and fulfillment will come only when you exercise the true gifts the Holy Spirit has placed within *you*. You and your gifts are like fingers in a perfectly fitted glove. God created you with a combination of gifts and qualities that no one else has. You are unique. And with His power, you can fulfill the role He has for you in the body of Christ.

Remember, too, that the "quiet" gifts may be the most essential of all. How will we ever get the details done unless someone uses the gift of helps? How will we find the resources without someone's gift of giving? We need each other. Someone with leadership is helpless without someone else who can administrate. The preacher is ineffective without believers who have the gifts of prayer, fasting, giving, and service. Use your true gift with a right understanding of its place in your life, and your place in ministry.

Finally, serve in response to the needs of others, regardless of your gifts. The Bible declares, "For you have been called to live in freedom—not freedom to satisfy your sinful nature, but freedom to serve one another in love" (Galatians 5:13). I believe that we as Christians should use our gifts without actually being gift-centered. There is a difference. We should be driven by needs rather than gifts, for as we identify the needs, our gifts emerge in ministry.

Jesus is the ultimate example of service. If Jesus had reasoned like most of us, he might have said something like this: "My time on earth is short, so I plan to focus on My gift of teaching. I will be needing plenty of time to Myself. I have some major sermons to prepare."

But that is not how Jesus behaved. He always found the time to encourage children and those who were overlooked by society. He constantly managed to stop to heal a sick person or attend dinner with someone shunned by society. He responded to the needs of both the haves and the have-nots. Jesus was not focused selfishly on Himself and His gifts, but on the needs of others. He said that He came to seek and to save those who were lost (Luke 19:10), and He lived totally for the needs of those around Him. Though He was God, Jesus humbled Himself, washed His disciples' feet, and took the worst imaginable punishment on our behalf because our greatest need of all was salvation.

Jesus said, "For even I, the Son of Man, came here not to be served but to serve others, and to give my life as a ransom for many" (Matthew 20:28). He should be our ultimate model for service.

Fulfillment Through Our Gifts

Serving in the power of the Holy Spirit will bring you the greatest fulfillment life has to offer. You are one piece of a great, worldwide jigsaw puzzle whose picture of the eternal body of Christ has yet to be completely assembled. There can be nothing more forlorn and useless than a puzzle piece that has fallen on the floor, been swept under the carpet, and separated from the rest of the puzzle. Without that one piece, the great picture can never be complete. The piece itself has no value. But when it is found, and when it settles into the puzzle with a satisfying click, all its shapes and colors suddenly fit with perfect precision. The puzzle piece interlocks properly on every side and helps to make a beautiful picture.

The use of gifts under the Spirit's direction is the missing piece to the puzzle of modern Christianity. The Bible gives us this admonition:

> God has given each of us the ability to do certain things well. So if God has given you the ability to prophesy, speak out when you have faith that God is speaking through you. If your gift is that of serving others, serve them well. If you are a teacher, do a good job of teaching. If your gift is to encourage others, do it! If you have money, share it generously. If God has given you leadership ability, take the responsibility seriously. And if you have a gift for showing kindness to others, do it gladly (Romans 12:6–8).

Let us try to imagine a church that took those words completely to heart. What would such a congregation be like? Think of it—every member busy using his or her gifts to build the fellowship, honor Christ, and reach nonbelievers. There would be teachers honing their skills to become very effective instructors in the Word. There would be people with the gift of helps pitching in to fill every need. Encouragers would be actively ministering to all the hurts in the congregation, and those with the gift of administration would have everything organized with perfect efficiency. Evangelists would be mobilizing the congregation to win the community to Christ, and when difficult decisions arose, those with the gift of wisdom would provide spiritual insight.

Such a church would truly be a "city on a hill" in that community, a lighthouse that would attract seekers from every direction. There would be little time for petty and divisive controversies, because miracles of grace would be on every side, to the delight of all. Christ would live, breathe, and bless the world through such a church. As a matter of fact, the world would flock to that church, almost beating down the doors. Members of lost humanity would see in that body of believers all that they longed for in life. They would see the pearl of great price, and give up all they had to be a part of it.

Find and exercise your spiritual gifts, and help all your fellow believers do the same.

I do not believe this is an idealistic pipe dream, but the very plan that God has for every church in this world. Too many of our congregations are struggling to justify their existence, to protect their slumping attendance, and much of that is because believers are not being led to use their gifts. The church is not ministering to needs. We can do better, and it can begin with you. Find and exercise your spiritual gifts, and help all your fellow believers do the same.

I believe that a major revival will begin when Christians take this mandate seriously. People will once again be won to the Lord in huge numbers—which brings us to our next chapter, concerning how the Spirit helps us to evangelize the lost.

Life Application

 Meditate on the Words of the Spirit. Make it a priority to memorize and meditate on the following verses:

- "For we are God's masterpiece. He has created us anew in Christ Jesus, so that we can do the good things He planned for us long ago" (Ephesians 2:10).

- "God has given gifts to each of you from His great variety of spiritual gifts. Manage them well so that God's generosity can flow through you" (1 Peter 4:10).

 Focus on the Presence of the Spirit. Search your heart as you ask these questions about your life:

- What spiritual gifts have others recognized in you through your service?

- How are you using your gifts to build up the body of Christ?

- What needs do you see in your church that you believe God wants you to meet?

 Walk in the Power of the Spirit. The Holy Spirit generously bestows spiritual gifts on believers in order to build up the church and glorify Christ. God wants you to be a part of Christ's plan for His church and the world! Commit yourself to practicing the truths in the GIFTS acrostic.

Give of your gifts in love through the power of the Holy Spirit.

Identify your gifts through the confirmation of others as you serve.

Fulfill God's purpose for your life by developing your gifts.

Think rightly about yourself and your gifts.

Serve in response to the need of others, regardless of your gifts.

Ask God today to help you make your gifts as effective as possible in building the church and glorifying Christ. If you have not identified your gift, work with church leaders to do so.

Chapter 11

Our Empowerment for Evangelism

I f we are truthful, we must admit that we are sometimes indifferent about the souls of certain people. There is that man who rudely honks his horn in traffic, the uncaring receptionist at the other end of a telephone line, the tiresome person ahead of us in line at the grocery store. We even have friends with whom we never attempt to discuss the most important news the world has ever heard—the news of Jesus Christ.

We know we should share the wonderful, life-changing news of the gospel, but we are afraid. We feel inadequate, or we think other things are more important. And, perhaps most of all, we lack the love that would compel us to share our faith. Meanwhile, God loves every single one of these lost, lonely people with an everlasting love. He desperately yearns to reach them.

But He yearns to reach them *through us.* God's way is to rescue people through other people. He has sprinkled us around the world to be "the salt of the earth" (Matthew 5:13), acting as a preservative against immorality. He has set us ablaze with His glory to be the "light of the world" (Matthew 5:14), illuminating the path to Jesus for others.

Our Most Important Task

How important is it that we share our faith? It was so important to Jesus that His final words to His disciples before He ascended to heaven were, "Go into all the world and preach the Good News to everyone, everywhere" (Mark 16:15). By making these His last words, Jesus underscored the priority He places on sharing the Good News with others. These are our marching orders—Job One for this lifetime.

As I have traveled the world for more than fifty years, I have asked millions of Christians two questions. First I ask, "What is the most important thing that has ever happened to you?" The response is almost always, "Receiving Jesus Christ as my Savior and Lord." Then I ask, "In light of that, what is the most important thing you can do with your life?" The answer? "Tell others how to receive Christ, too."

But how do people know they need Christ? The truth is that many people seem to have no awareness that they are completely lost. As a young man, I was a "happy pagan" under the impression that I already had all the fulfillment life had to offer. I did not know that I was a sinner, desperately in need of the Savior. But Christ came to embark on a rescue mission, to go out and find every wandering soul and restore them to heaven. Jesus declared, "I, the Son of Man, have come to seek and save those like him who are lost" (Luke 19:10).

Of course, Jesus walked the earth for only a few years. Time and geography limited the numbers He could reach. But through the wonderful power of the Holy Spirit, Jesus Christ still reaches out to lost sinners. He wants to do so through you and me.

Many Christians believe that evangelism is one small part of our faith, or that it is a particular gift for those who are called to it. But we know two things from the Great Commission: witnessing is at the very heart of our faith, and it is for everyone. Paul writes to the Corinthians, "We are Christ's ambassadors, and God is using us to speak to you. We urge you, as though Christ Himself were here pleading with you, 'Be reconciled to God!'" (2 Corinthians 5:20).

Therefore, we should share our faith as full-time ambassadors, and with the urgency of Christ Himself speaking through us. That is exactly what He is doing.

The Burden of Eternity

The Great Commission to introduce others to Christ is not just a suggestion from our Lord, it is a command. It is no small thing to carry on our shoulders the burden of others' eternal destiny. All around us are people who could die at any time and face an eternity of punishment and separation from God, simply because no one told them the wonderful news of salvation. Many of us live through years and decades without sharing our faith with people who work beside us, go to school with us, or live next door.

Yes, the burden of someone else's eternal destiny, heaven or hell, is an awesome responsibility. Yet it should not be considered a burdensome task. We should look upon sharing our faith as the greatest of joys. Indeed, if it is the Holy Spirit who witnesses through us, who prods us to speak and gives us the words, then we should feel the same joy that He feels. I have met countless Christians who have told me that they had never realized how thrilling and satisfying it was to be used by God to lead a friend to Christ.

We witness because our hearts are motivated by joy and our wills are motivated by obedience.

We witness because our hearts are motivated by joy and our wills are motivated by obedience. Jesus said, "Therefore, go and make disciples of all the nations, baptizing them in the name of the Father and the Son and the Holy Spirit" (Matthew 28:19). This is a command of Christ, and the one which I take to be the greatest one of all. We are to go and make disciples. We must obey and obey joyfully.

As we move forward to share our witness, we need never fear. Christ sent us with this promise: "And be sure of this: I am with you always, even to the end of the age" (Matthew 28:20).

This promise, my friend, is all you need. If the Spirit chooses to speak through you, you should have no hesitation in being obedient in sharing your faith.

The Spirit Gives Us Power

Jesus said, "When the Holy Spirit has come upon you, you will receive power and will tell people about Me everywhere—in Jerusalem, throughout Judea, in Samaria, and to the ends of the earth" (Acts 1:8).

155

We cannot fail to notice that in both Matthew 28:19,20 and Acts 1:8, Jesus emphasizes the empowerment of the Spirit for our witnessing. I believe that if more Christians realized the implications of this truth, there would be much less fear and hesitation over sharing our faith. We go not in our own power, but in the Spirit's.

If the Spirit did not speak through you, you would be unlikely to have any success leading others to Christ. But because He promises to be with you "always, even to the end of the age," you can be confident of your ability to share your faith successfully.

Add this promise from Jesus to His disciples: "Now I will send the Holy Spirit, just as my Father promised. But stay here in the city until the Holy Spirit comes and fills you with power from heaven" (Luke 24:49). Is it not interesting that pending the arrival of the Spirit, Jesus actually restrained His disciples from going out into the world and sharing their faith? Without His enabling, all our efforts would be in vain; with Him, we can turn the world upside down.

Peter's transformation at Pentecost is a dramatic example of what happens when a person is filled with the heavenly power of God's Spirit. When Jesus was arrested, Peter publicly denied Him three times (John 18:17–27). Yet only a short time later, Peter preached a sermon so powerful that three thousand people became believers in one day (Acts 2:14–41). How is it that a man cowers before a servant girl one day, then preaches one of history's most powerful sermons a few days later? There is only one answer—through the magnificent power of the Holy Spirit! My friend, whatever your self-doubts may be when it comes to personal witnessing, you can be no less confident than Peter was as he denied His Savior and friend of three years. But you can witness with every bit of the power Peter demonstrated when three thousand souls responded to his sermon and entered the kingdom of God. The same Spirit who filled Peter lives within you if you are a born-again follower of Christ.

Recently I have been involved in launching the Global Pastor's Network to train millions of laymen and professional leaders to start house churches. We have divided the world's six billion people into six thousand Million Population Target Areas (MPTAs), and we are asking individuals and churches to adopt one MPTA as a means to plant thousands of house churches in each area. What a phenomenal impact this will have around the world. It takes boldness to send ordinary people into the middle of crowded urban jungles where there is so much sin. But each one of our leaders is able to appropriate the power of the Holy Spirit, and we have every confidence that miracles will happen, strongholds will be taken down, and millions of lost people will come into the kingdom of our dear Lord Jesus Christ.

Without the Spirit, we would have no boldness or confidence. But we can do all things through Him who strengthens us.

The Spirit Persuades and Convicts

There is a great misconception about evangelism: people believe it has something to do with winning an argument. Naturally, arguing is the worst way to convince someone of anything. Pride becomes involved, two sides square off, and it is unlikely that anyone will leave with a changed mind. Certainly when it comes to witnessing, we need not argue or contend with people intellectually. No one is ever debated into the kingdom of God. It is our role to practice gentle persuasion, and it is the Holy Spirit who does the persuading. He works in the hearts and minds of the people to whom we witness. He bursts through mental barriers to convict people of the truth.

Many years ago, I was a counselor at one of Billy Graham's Los Angeles crusades held in the Hollywood Bowl. At the end of the meeting, another counselor brought a man to me who was an engineer. The engineer stated that if I could answer his questions, he would become a Christian. I asked him if he wanted to know Christ. He said he did. I suggested that he pray and receive Christ and then we would discuss his questions. Amazingly, he agreed. After we prayed, I asked to hear his questions. He looked at me with a smile and said, "I don't have any questions. They are all answered."

The real issue with nonbelievers is usually not an intellectual one; it is an issue of the will. It is the role of the Holy Spirit to break down that barrier and provide all the answers. As Paul wrote, "We know these things because God has revealed them to us by His Spirit, and His Spirit searches out everything and shows us even God's deep secrets" (1 Corinthians 2:10).

We can be certain that the Spirit will remove an individual's barriers of doubt. But He does something else as well: He convicts people of their sin and their need for salvation. We often worry about how we can persuade a nonbeliever to be saved from his sin when he refuses to acknowledge the existence of sin. Again, this work of persuasion is not our responsibility but the work of the Holy Spirit. Anyone who has ever shared his faith can attest to the powerful conviction that often fills one who is confronted by the gospel. There is a sudden, overpowering awareness of the reality of sin; a person suddenly sees himself through new eyes. There are often tears, remorse, and a tremendous desire for immediate salvation.

> *If the Spirit can work within the mind of the friend to whom you are witnessing, He can work inside you, too.*

We simply need to take God at His Word that the Spirit will accomplish His work in the hearts and minds of those to whom we witness. God proclaimed through the prophet Isaiah, "It is the same with My word. I send it out, and it always produces fruit. It will accomplish all I want it to, and it will prosper everywhere I send it" (Isaiah 55:11). In short, God is sovereign. If He desires to reach out to someone with the gospel through you or me, He will do so. It is our responsibility to go and share God's love and plan of salvation.

The Spirit Provides the Right Words

But how will we know what to say? I often hear reluctant witnesses saying, "My tongue would be tied if I shared my faith. I would have no idea what to say!"

If the Spirit can work within the mind of the friend to whom you are witnessing, He can work inside you, too. When salvation is on the line, be certain that the Spirit will provide you with just the right words to say to your friend. Over the years I have often smiled as younger Christians have told me, "It was as if someone else was doing the talking! I had no idea I could share my faith like that—the right words just kept coming." Someone else *was* doing the talking. It will

158

be your lips, your mouth, and your voice, but the Spirit will guide your conversation in just the direction it should go. You need only be open to His leadership. Before you share your faith, always have a private word of prayer first. Ask God to forgive you of any unconfessed sin and fill you with His Spirit. He will give you the right words every time.

Listen to what Jesus told His disciples as He spoke of their future: "But when you are arrested and stand trial, don't worry about what to say in your defense. Just say what God tells you to. Then it is not you who will be speaking, but the Holy Spirit" (Mark 13:11). The Bible gives many instances of how this happened to Peter, Paul, Stephen, and others. Some of the most powerful sermons in history were delivered when Christians were arrested by Roman authorities. Read the Book of Acts closely and you will see that this book might well have been called "The Acts of the Spirit," for all the power in the early church came through Him, as it still does today.

The Spirit will speak through you, and He will always use Scripture as His sword to penetrate a person's soul and spirit. I hope you will always have your Bible with you when you share your faith, even if it is a small New Testament that fits in your pocket. Take some time to learn the key verses for sharing your faith. And never worry in advance about whether your friend accepts the Bible as His authority. This is irrelevant; what matters is that the Spirit accepts the Word and uses it powerfully. The truth will cut through with precision, as the writer of Hebrews reminds us: "The word of God is full of living power. It is sharper than the sharpest knife, cutting deep into our innermost thoughts and desires. It exposes us for what we really are" (Hebrews 4:12).

Many years ago, as I thought of the best way I could present the gospel, I outlined "Four Spiritual Laws" and used Scripture verses with each of them. Over the decades, the Spirit has used this simple presentation to help tens of millions of believers lead others to Christ. I recommend that you refer to these laws, listed in Appendix B, and use them as a starting place in your witnessing opportunities. And remember that the Spirit of God will always use the Word of God in tugging at the heart of a nonbeliever.

Preparing in the Spirit

I have often made this statement: *I have never led anyone to Christ, and I never will.*

Those words invariably cause a few uplifted eyebrows, which settle back down when my listeners realize the words are literally true: it is not me but the Holy Spirit who does the leading—all of it—and it is He who has given me the privilege of praying with thousands of people as they received Christ. No one can experience salvation unless it is through the work of the Holy Spirit.

What a relief to know that it is the Holy Spirit who is responsible for producing fruit. We simply take the initiative to share Christ in the power of the Holy Spirit and leave the results to God. You will remember that Edward Kimball felt inadequate and unsuccessful when he shared his faith with Moody. Yet indirectly, his simple obedience led to hundreds of millions of conversions up to this day.

In the remainder of this chapter, I would like to leave you with seven directives on witnessing that I have found helpful over the years.

First, *walk in a manner that demonstrates honorable character and the Spirit-filled life.* Your character must be above reproach. There will be times when you stumble. But in every way possible, you must ask the Holy Spirit to help you be a person of integrity capable of bringing as much honor as possible to the gospel. The Bible tells us, "But whatever happens to me, you must live in a manner worthy of the Good News about Christ, as citizens of heaven" (Philippians 1:27). This does not mean that an admirable spiritual lifestyle is a sufficient witness; you must also be proactive in opening your mouth and sharing the gospel. But an impure life will greatly damage your witness. It has been said that your life is the first Bible some people will ever read. Please avoid letting it become a barrier to their reading the true one.

Second, *intercede for the lost in prayer.* Too many Christians live out a lukewarm faith today, often because they are not sharing their faith in Christ with others. If they are not sharing their faith, it is because they lack a true burden for nonbelievers. If they lack a burden for the lost, it is because they lack the love that would result in such a burden. And if they lack that love, surely it is because they have not been praying daily for these people.

The apostle Paul felt deeply for those who did not know Jesus as Savior. He prayed with special zeal for his fellow Jews. In the book of Romans, Paul wrote, "Dear brothers and sisters, the longing of my heart and my prayer to God is that the Jewish people might be saved" (Romans 10:1).

My friend, for whom are you praying daily? Do you remember to pray for the salvation of your loved ones, neighbors, and friends? Your supervisor at work? Your unreached cousin? The struggling single parent three houses down? If you have lacked the will to go and share Christ with these people, do you lack the will to pray for them? Bring their names before God daily and see if He does not give you the desire and the strength to share Christ's love and forgiveness with them.

Witnessing in the Spirit

Third, *take the initiative to present the gospel.* When will that defining moment finally come about? It is up to you. We are told that when the explorer David Livingstone shared his faith with a tribal leader in Africa, the leader asked him a piercing question. If the lost must face eternal punishment, he asked, why had it taken so long for Livingstone's country to send a messenger?

Imagine leading your neighbor to Christ, seeing his tears of joy, then having to answer that question. With salvation and forgiveness so transforming and wonderful, life in Christ so abundant and joyful, fellowship with other believers so full and rewarding, why have we waited? Why have we risked seeing someone die suddenly without hearing the incredible news of the gospel? The conclusion is inescapable: we must take the initiative and present the gospel at every opportunity.

The best place to begin is right in your own home. Jesus told the first Christians to begin their witness in Jerusalem, where they lived. Note the pattern in how Jesus instructed us to share the gospel: "in Jerusalem, throughout Judea, in Samaria, and to the ends of the earth" (Acts 1:8). You might paraphrase it this way: in your hometown, across your state and territory, and over the seas to every inhabited town and village. But it begins right where you stand, and it begins with those within the sound of your voice and the touch of your hand. Reach out to those people, then see how far your reach will finally extend. Edward Kimball never knew the full scope of his witness to Moody. He spoke quietly in a shoe store, and his words echoed to the ends of the earth, just as Jesus promised.

Fourth, *never argue, but show loving concern.* God never desires for you to get caught up in words that divide—this is obviously the game of your adversary, the devil. Remember to trust the Spirit, who is so much more powerful than Satan. Remember to love and to listen. Keep to God's Word, which will be empowered by the Spirit, and avoid tangential questions.

Fifth, *expect the Holy Spirit to lead you to receptive people.* I am constantly alert to see who God will send across my path. Some years ago

Keep to God's Word, which will be empowered by the Spirit, and avoid tangential questions.

I was stranded at the St. Louis airport after a conference. Poor weather conditions had led to all flights being canceled. I was weary and discouraged. But as in all times of disappointment, I fixed my mind on Romans 8:28: "We know that all that happens to us is working for our good if we love God and are fitting into His plans" (TLB) and 1 Thessalonians 5:18: "Give thanks in all circumstances, for this is God's will for you in Christ Jesus." God had His reasons for the delay, and I was thankful in the midst of it.

Arriving back in the lobby of the hotel, I immediately met a businessman who was clearly hungry for God. I explained to my new friend how to receive Christ, and together we knelt and prayed. With great joy he entered the family of God. As we finished praying, my new brother in Christ beamed a smile that could light up an auditorium and asked, "What do you do for a living?" I told him that I travel the world, sharing Christ with anyone who will listen. Then he made a statement I shall never forget: "You must bring a lot of happiness into this world."

I went to bed that night with a wide smile of my own, singing praises to God because I knew it was true: I have the privilege of bringing a lot of happiness into this world. So do you and every believer. And since that is true, are you not eager for God to bring you people who need that happiness found only through faith in our Lord?

Sharing, Speaking, and Sowing

Sixth, *share what God has done for you*. God's Word proclaims, "You are a kingdom of priests, God's holy nation, His very own possession. This is so you can show others the goodness of God, for He called you out of the darkness into His wonderful light" (1 Peter 2:9). This verse tells me that all that I have, all that God has done for me, every good thing I possess, was given so that I can demonstrate the goodness of God. This little light of mine, in other words, is there so that it might shine in a darkened world. One thing no one can argue about is what God has done for you. I challenge you to prepare your personal three-minute testimony. Use the simple three-point outline of what your life was like before you met Christ, how you received Christ, and what your life has been like ever since.

Share the wonderful things He has done for you. You are the living proof of the redemptive power of God, so be certain that your witness is warm and personal. Your listeners cannot help responding to the light that glows from your life and experience.

Finally, three further suggestions: *Speak boldly, stay on track, and seek the Holy Spirit's guidance in your conversation*. I believe that if you keep these three simple S-words in mind, your witness is sure to be compelling and fruitful. You speak boldly because you come as an ambassador for Christ, a spokesman for the Creator of this universe. You stay on track because, compared to what you have to say, any other subject would be trivial and inconsequential. And you seek the Spirit's guidance because with such a Guide, there are no wrong turns to be taken, no poor words to be chosen, no lack of wisdom or discernment to possibly bring a shadow across your encounter.

Is it not wonderful to consider that the very Spirit of God lives within you and seeks to make Christ known in every corner of the globe through you? What other activity could you possibly prefer to being a vessel of the holy, perfect Savior, doing the greatest work that life has to offer, bearing fruit that will last for all eternity? After more than half a century, that thought still makes my heart race. I cannot wait to share the gospel with everyone who will listen—and trust the results to the One who is in control.

Remember, it is your task to sow the seeds wherever possible. You cannot control where the seeds land, nor whether they take root. When Vonette and I were first ministering at UCLA, many students came to know the Lord. But sometimes I would hear about a student whom I had discipled for months returning to the old lifestyle, and I would be tremendously discouraged. Had I not shared the gospel correctly? Did it not "take"?

God answered my prayer by showing me the parable of the sower (Mark 4:15–20). In that story, a man sowed the earth with seeds that fell in various places. They fell either on a hardened path, rocky soil, thorny ground, or good soil. Jesus explained that just as there are plots of earth, some suitable and some less so—there are souls in the same condition. Within some people, the gospel never takes root. In others, the devil snatches away the seeds of faith before they can break out. But there are some whose souls are fertile for the gospel to grow and flourish. You cannot determine the receptivity of another person's heart. You can only be faithful to distribute the seed as carefully and lovingly as possible.

Long ago I learned that it is unproductive for me to spend time worrying about those who have heard and rejected the gospel. I can only be responsible for the presentation. Though I must do everything I can to help new believers grow and mature in their faith, I praise God that the Holy Spirit, who helps me to witness clearly and powerfully, will do the work of growth in those individuals. Perhaps the seed will not germinate until tomorrow. Perhaps it will break the soil next year or next decade. Only the Lord knows, and it would be arrogant for me to demand the answers.

We are merely the sowers, you and I. We must engage in what I have called for many years "spiritual multiplication." This concept is simply winning people to Christ, building them in their Christian faith, then sending them out to win and disciple others for our Lord Jesus, generation after generation. Let us sow abundantly—enabled by the power of the Holy Spirit, whose love and grace will do a miraculous work.

In the next chapter we will discuss the ministry of the Spirit through the high and low times of our lives.

Life Application

 Meditate on the Words of the Spirit. Commit the following verses to memory:

- "When the Holy Spirit has come upon you, you will receive power and will tell people about Me everywhere—in Jerusalem, throughout Judea, in Samaria, and to the ends of the earth" (Acts 1:8).

- "My true disciples produce much fruit. This brings great glory to My Father" (John 15:8).

 Focus on the Presence of the Spirit. Contemplate the following questions:

- When was the last time you told someone about your relationship with Jesus?

- Why is witnessing difficult for you? What motivates you to share your faith?

- What areas of your life need to conform more to the image of Christ?

 Walk in the Power of the Spirit. Many believers are uncomfortable with telling others about Jesus. But if we do not speak about the life-giving message of the gospel, we are allowing our fears and insecurities to keep people from getting right with God and inheriting eternal life! The stakes are too high to listen to our fears and excuses. Follow the steps in the WITNESS acrostic to become a vibrant, courageous advocate for Christ.

Walk in a manner that demonstrates honorable character and the Spirit-filled life.

Intercede for the lost in prayer.

Take the initiative to present the Gospel.

Never argue, but show loving concern.

Expect the Holy Spirit to lead you to receptive people.

Share what God has done for you.

Speak boldly, stay on track, and seek the Holy Spirit's guidance in your conversation.

Ask God to give you an opportunity to share your faith today, and to fill you with His Spirit as you share the most wonderful news life has to offer.

Chapter 12

Our Counselor for Decision-Making

Jim was an executive with a telephone company. He worked hard and built a good reputation, right up to the day that his division closed. The company had no desire to lose a fine employee like Jim, so they offered him a transfer to a branch in another state. For extra incentive, he could look forward to a hefty pay raise if he made the move.

Jim faced one of those agonizing decisions in life. He was a committee chairman and taught Sunday school at a church where the family had grown in their love for Christ. His wife had many friends and activities. Then there were the children, who were settled comfortably in their school. Pulling them out and moving them in the middle of the academic year would be a lot to ask of them.

Still, that promotion was worth considering—and he could use the pay raise. Jim decided to accept the offer and put his house up for sale. He and his wife began making all the busy preparations involved in a cross-country move, saying their good-byes and tying up loose ends. But as the move date approached, the couple's nagging feeling only intensified. This decision had not brought a moment of real peace—for either of them.

"That's when we started praying," Jim said with a slightly embarrassed laugh. "Here I was a church leader, and I had forgotten to ask God what He wanted." Jim and his wife agreed to pray for guidance, and both of them came to the conclusion that the Holy Spirit did not want them to make the move. This made nothing easier, of course; now Jim had no job. He decided that if God did not want the move,

He must have some other plan. There was nothing to do but to trust God and see what transpired.

Several months later, Jim heard that the phone company had closed the division in the other state. If he had taken that job, he would have given up so many good things only to be stranded and jobless.

Have you ever been faced with a difficult decision, one where there seemed to be no right or easy answer? Have you wished the solution was written neatly in the clouds or listed for quick reference in a book somewhere? No one relishes making a significant decision when the important things in life are on the line.

Just the same, we all face those anxious moments. As Christians, we can rest in the assurance that we are never as isolated as we feel at decision time. We have the Spirit to come alongside us, encourage us, empower us, and help us make the right decision. "For I know the plans I have for you," says the LORD. "They are plans for good and not for disaster, to give you a future and a hope" (Jeremiah 29:11). Could any words be more reassuring? God knows the future already; it is not one of chance and chaos, but one defined by His perfect plan, lovingly worked out with our welfare in mind.

That does not mean we will always choose the right path in accordance with that perfect plan. We are fallen human beings, born again of the Spirit yet prey to the weakness of the flesh. We often choose impulsively. We decide without taking the Spirit's counsel or with an incorrect interpretation of it. The plan of God is perfect, but the steps of people are often faulty. Even the wisest of Christians have wandered from the right path at some time or another. So what should we do?

Hearing His Voice

The solution, of course, is to learn to discern clearly the voice of the Master. Jesus compared Himself to a good shepherd leading the flock: "When he has brought out all his own, he goes on ahead of them, and his sheep follow him because they know his voice" (John 10:4, NIV). We must come to a humble realization that we are sheep who need a shepherd for every step. The landscape is full of deep pits and hungry wolves, and we need to be led toward the green pastures and quiet waters the Shepherd desires for us. We must know His voice and follow it obediently.

Be assured that the Lord wants to lead you even more than you want to follow Him. The Good Shepherd would never hide from His sheep or lead them into a dangerous place. God is eager for you to hear His voice, and you need only have the desire to follow it. Hearing God's voice is not only important for knowing the *general* plan that applies to all believers—abiding in prayer, studying the Word, living in purity, and so on—but also for knowing the *personal* plan that God has for each individual believer.

For instance, you need not grapple with the question of whether to marry a nonbeliever; we know from the Word of God that this is forbidden to any of us. But you will need to confront the issue of whether to marry this Christian or that one, for this falls under the category of His *personal* plan for you.

> *We must come to a*
>
> *humble realization*
>
> *that we are sheep*
>
> *who need a shepherd*
>
> *for every step.*

My good friend and spiritual mentor from many years ago, Henrietta Mears, provides a good example of these ideas. Early on, it was her firm conviction that God would call her to go overseas as a missionary. But she was not blessed with good eyesight. She recognized that this infirmity would be an obstacle to her service overseas. In time she realized the call to missions was not forthcoming from God. Meanwhile, she was growing to love a young man who was not a believer. Because he was not a Christian, Miss Mears had to break off the engagement. The issue of her personal vocation was difficult, and it clarified only over time; the issue of marriage, in this case, was simple and general. She recognized that she could not be unequally yoked with a nonbeliever.

Ultimately Dr. Mears ended up in Southern California, where she became the Director of Christian Education at the First Presbyterian Church of Hollywood. From that position she had a global impact. She certainly had a tremendous influence on Vonette and me, as well as Richard Halverson (who would become Chaplain of the United States Senate), Billy Graham, and thousands of others. She founded

Gospel Light Publications, impacting Christian literature worldwide. She also founded Forrest Home Christian Conference Center, where hundreds of thousands have experienced new life in Christ. But she had to be patient and obedient as God worked out His perfect will for her. We might say that her physical vision was limited, but her spiritual vision was far-reaching.

Step by step, God lays out His special plan for each of us. That has certainly been my personal experience in ministry. Perhaps we would be terrified if we could see the big picture from the very beginning. In His perfect time, God shows us what He wants us to see. We may be interested in the details of the plan, but He is always interested in the details of the relationship as we depend on Him daily.

In our souls we may be saying, "Just tell me, Lord! I cannot wait— I want to know now!" But the gentle voice of the Spirit replies, *Be patient. Know Me well, and the future will take care of itself. We will work it out together, you and I, if you will simply trust Me.*

The Word, Prayer, and Providence

So how does the Spirit guide us toward the correct decision?

The most common way is through His Word. The Bible is the yardstick we must use to measure all other forms of guidance. The Holy Spirit will never lead us down a path contrary to the Word, God's direct, universal revelation. He does not change, and neither does His Word. The psalmist declared, "Your word is a lamp for my feet and a light for my path" (Psalm 119:105). Most of our important decisions would be far easier if we would only read, understand, and obey the Scriptures.

As we read the Word, the Spirit will also guide us through prayer. If you really believe in the power of prayer, you will know that He plans to grant your request for guidance. You will talk to God, but more importantly, you will listen for His voice. Pray consistently about any matter and I believe you will find guidance. James tells us that this is really very simple: "If you need wisdom—if you want to know what God wants you to do—ask Him, and He will gladly tell you. He will not resent your asking" (James 1:5).

After examining the Word and committing to prayer, we can look for the Spirit to guide us in a third way: through providential circumstances. We must take great care in reading the events around us, but there are times when we can discern the voice of God speaking through the circumstances of life.

Many years ago, I was driving in the mountains when my car started to heat up. I noticed a ranger station and stopped to ask for water for my car. I loosened my radiator cap, and it blew sky high. As I stooped to pick up the cap, a New Testament fell out of my breast pocket. After replacing both, I drove away. Obviously God was trying to say something to me. I listened to God and received a strong impression: He wanted me to speak to the ranger. So I turned the car around and headed back.

When I returned to his station, the ranger came out to greet me. He asked if I had forgotten something. I told him indeed I had; I had forgotten to talk to him about Jesus. The ranger was very receptive, and he eventually explained to me that there had been a time when he was a pillar in his church. Somewhere along the way, however, a negative spirit had taken root in him. He had given in to bitterness and had not gone to church for years. That day, the ranger and I got on our knees as he confessed his sin. God's joy was restored to his life.

For the ranger, my appearance at his station was a providential event. For me, the Bible falling from my pocket was one. Be wise and discerning as you interpret the flow of events in your life, but know that God uses all things for His purposes.

Counsel, Common Sense, and Convictions

No believer should ever make an important decision without seeking godly counsel from a respected man or woman of God. This may be a pastor, a church elder, a Bible study leader, or anyone who has walked intimately with God over many years.

Solomon, who happened to be the wisest man of all time, reminds us, "Plans go wrong for lack of advice; many counselors bring success" (Proverbs 15:22). I have mentioned that Henrietta Mears was an early counselor who helped me consider decisions of life and ministry. Over time, I myself have given advice to thousands of younger believers. When we seek other perspectives, we are likely to see our situation in an entirely new way. Godly counselors are sent by the Lord to open our eyes to all the issues.

The Spirit will also lead us through what I call "sanctified common sense." Many years ago, God helped me grasp this concept when I was reflecting upon the following verse: "God has not given us a spirit of fear, but of power and of love and of a sound mind" (2 Timothy 1:7, NKJ). The "sound mind" referred to in this verse means a well-balanced mind, a mind that is under the control of the Holy Spirit. (See "How to Know God's Will" in Appendix D.)

This is an important verse, for it tells us that a sound mind, which we might think of as plain common sense, is a gift of the Spirit in the same way that love and power come from Him. There may be times when we feel God has not spoken clearly, when we would prefer to delay and continue seeking God, but an immediate decision must be made. In such cases, we should use rational thinking grounded in the truths of God's Word. God has given His children the "mind of Christ" (1 Corinthians 2:16), and that means if we put Him first and seek to honor Him, He will direct our decisions.

Any prompting we receive from the Holy Spirit will always honor God and be faithful to Scripture.

The Holy Spirit also guides us through inner impressions or promptings. When the Bible fell from my pocket that day at the ranger station, it was a providential experience. But as I sought God's guidance, the decision to speak to the ranger about his soul came from an inner prompting. This is subjective, of course. New believers should take great caution in discerning that "still, small voice." As we grow in the knowledge of God's Word, we find that we become increasingly sensitive to the Holy Spirit's leading. It helps to remember that any prompting we receive from the Holy Spirit will always honor God and be faithful to Scripture.

When I was a new Christian, the Holy Spirit impressed me to visit the president of one of the largest oil companies in the world. I was very uncomfortable with the outrageous idea of walking into the office of such an important man, but I felt I must be obedient to God's leadership. I was amazed when the tycoon immediately agreed to see me. As I arrived at his office, he asked, "What can I do for you, young man?" I got right to the point and asked him about his relationship with Jesus Christ.

God had clearly ordained this appointment. This powerful business leader sitting in front of me began to weep. He had received Christ as a young boy but had spent his entire adult life pursuing success. As he had gained the world, he felt that he had lost his soul. His wife, his children, particularly His Lord—he wanted them all back in his life. We wept together. As I stood to leave, he told me that he had not been in a church for thirty years, and that he intended to change that pattern on the following Sunday.

I left his office rejoicing that I had obeyed the prompting of the Holy Spirit. God is so faithful, and we need only be attentive and sensitive.

Supernatural Manifestations

We need to consider one further possibility for the Spirit's leadership. He will occasionally use supernatural manifestations such as dreams, visions, angels, or even an appearance of Christ Himself to guide us. These experiences happened in Bible times, and they happen today in various parts of the world.

God spoke to Jacob and Joseph in dreams. He revealed future events to prophets such as Daniel and Ezekiel through visions. An angel appeared to Mary, the mother of Jesus, and to the shepherds. The risen Lord Jesus stunned Paul on the Damascus Road. Let us be clear in affirming that these supernatural events are rare exceptions to God's usual methods of leading us. Nearly all of our decisions can be made simply by dwelling in the Word, abiding in prayer, using a sound mind, and consulting godly counsel. But there is no reason to limit God simply because we do not fully understand His ways. There are times when His name is glorified in ways that are more uncommon.

Most Muslims reside in countries where it is tremendously difficult or even fatal to talk about Jesus. Like everyone else, Muslims come to Christ most often because of the witness of a friend. But the second leading reason they become believers is due to a vision, a dream, or some supernatural phenomenon. Islam has a well-developed doctrine of angels and visions, and since Muslims are sensitive to those phenomena, God uses those events to draw them to Himself.[1]

Do these more dramatic dreams and visions happen in our own Christian environment? I am certain they do. I have known believers who have felt God's leading in that way. But the reason we should be very hesitant to expect such manifestations is that we know God leads us more often through the quietness of all the things that constitute our relationship with Him—the daily disciplines of prayer and Bible study. We might long for something more exciting, but God longs for us to grow in faith and maturity. That kind of growth comes through steadfast faith and obedience. As we learn to make decisions that please Him, we grow into people who please Him.

Did you realize that there are so many ways in which God can reveal His will to us? There are even many more than those I have listed. Finding His perfect will is no simple matter, for it touches on the complexity of His ordered creation. The world and the billions of lives within it are a great tapestry He has woven, and your decisions affect the lives and decisions of many other people—all while God, who knows the future and everything else, is using all things for our good as we seek to glorify Him. For now, we can only see in a mirror dimly. But the time will come when we wake up in that perfect world of paradise and have all our questions answered. Then we will know all the answers to the great enigmas that plagued us in this life, and we will laugh at the sheer wisdom of God in His lovingkindness.

Until then, we must walk by faith and not by sight. That is the adventure He has chosen for us.

Preparing Yourself to Hear God

We have considered the many ways God may guide us. We should pay the most attention to the common and trustworthy ones, but be aware that He can speak to us in many different ways. The following eight directives provide the best counsel I can offer you in making godly decisions through the leadership of the Holy Spirit.

First, *ground yourself in the truth of God's Word.* Let the Scriptures be the place where you go for refreshment, growth, and the sheer joy of knowing that God speaks to all generations through these words. As you dwell in the Scriptures as a lifetime discipline, you will find that decision-making becomes less of a chore. So many of our questions are already answered in this book; so much of God's will is already spelled out for us.

From my lifetime of experience I urge you wholeheartedly to memorize key passages and let them take root within you, transforming your mind and your heart. I could never count the many times that some part of the Word has welled up within me at a crucial moment, before I could make a wrong decision or speak a word that might be displeasing to God. Let the Word dwell in you richly and you will be in a position to test any desire, impulse, or advice against the eternal Scriptures. I cannot say this strongly enough: test everything against the Word. Satan is always hoping to deceive believers. But it is far more difficult for him to lead you astray if you spend time reading, studying, and memorizing Scripture as a way of life.

The apostle Paul reminds us, "All Scripture is inspired by God and is useful to teach us what is true and to make us realize what is wrong in our lives. It straightens us out and teaches us to do what is right. It is God's way of preparing us in every way, fully equipped for every good thing God wants us to do" (2 Timothy 3:16,17). That recommendation is good enough for me. I hope you take it seriously.

Second, *use devotional time to listen to the Holy Spirit's leading.* The most important part of our time with God is not what we say but what we hear and sense. Ask questions of the Lord and learn to discern His responses. Many believers keep a prayer journal, which can be an extremely rewarding and faith-building experience. Record answers to your requests and petitions as well as what God is teaching you and how He is personally leading you. Young believers struggle in this area at times. They ask, "Why do I not hear God's voice? How will I know I am not imagining what He says?"

I can only tell you that in time you will come to recognize His voice as a farmer learns to interpret the weather signs. Jesus told His disciples, "My sheep listen to My voice; I know them, and they follow Me" (John 10:27, NIV). Little lambs may not know the shepherd's voice quite as well. They will stumble along and need a nudge from sheep who are more mature. But God will not hide from you. Live daily a crucified, Spirit-filled life, totally surrendered to the One who created you, loves you, and died for you. Be patient, keep seeking, and you will learn to hear His voice.

Discernment, Dedication, and Direction

Third, *interpret Scripture passages, circumstances, and impressions carefully*. I have counseled you to take note of all the many ways that God speaks—particularly through His Word, prayer, your own sound mind, and the wise counsel of others. Decisions balanced on all these factors will seldom be the wrong ones.

Many of us are too hasty to rationalize our desires. For example, a church elder leaves his wife saying that he knows God wants him to be happy. First of all, he would never find a Bible teaching to justify that plan—desertion of a marriage for personal gratification. In honest prayer, he would never receive that direction from God, who never contradicts His own Word. I would hope that godly counselors would not steer him in that direction. If the elder takes the counsel of all the methods we have discussed in this chapter, I believe he will do the right thing and protect his marriage.

Fourth, *decide to surrender your will to God continually*. Why do we hesitate to lay all our desires before the One who desires nothing but good for us? It can only be a matter of trust. Consider a young woman who is trying to select a career. She is a bright young lady and has many options open to her. But she is afraid to ask God which career path she should choose. Deep down she worries that He will immediately brand her as a missionary and put her on a boat bound for distant seas. Or perhaps He will give her some dull career she would never choose for herself.

That young woman should think about her concept of God. The God I serve loves me, and He knew even before I was born just how I should spend my life. He has designed me and gifted me for a specific career, so that I would feel the most joy and fulfillment by choosing what He has wanted for me all along. If God wants this young lady to become a missionary, He will plant a deep desire within her in accor-

dance with His will. If we trust God's character, we will submit ourselves totally to His will. Submit yourself as Paul commends us to do:

> I plead with you to give your bodies to God. Let them be a liv-
> ing and holy sacrifice—the kind He will accept. When you think
> of what He has done for you, is this too much to ask? Don't copy
> the behavior and customs of this world, but let God transform you
> into a new person by changing the way you think. Then you will
> know what God wants you to do, and you will know how good
> and pleasing and perfect His will really is (Romans 12:1,2).

Fifth, *ask the Holy Spirit daily for wisdom and direction*. God's Word
promises us, "If any of you lacks wisdom, he should ask God, who
gives generously to all without finding fault, and it will be given to
him" (James 1:5, NIV). Do you believe that God wants you to stumble
along in life, bereft of any guidance for doing the right thing? He
would never entrust the building of His kingdom to such a system.

How many of your decisions, great and small, do you think the
Holy Spirit wants to be involved in? Answer: *all of them*. He wants to
partner with you in making your life as fruitful and fulfilling as possible. He never desires that you make a single wrong decision. I hope
you will do as I do—stop in the midst of any crucial moment during
the day and ask the Spirit to give you wisdom and direction. The
Bible tells us we are to "pray without ceasing" (1 Thessalonians 5:17,
NKJ). See how different your life will become when you begin depending upon His guidance throughout the day.

Counsel, Confession, and Confidence

Sixth, *note the counsel of godly advisors*. I think of them as being like
God's messengers. Often they will give you advice that might save you
from months or years of disappointment and heartache. At the very
least, it should give you pause when a trusted advisor counsels against
the thing you are strongly considering. No matter how great your
eagerness, you should stop and give the decision more time, simply
because a wise person's advice is worth taking seriously. God can
speak directly through our mentors and trusted friends. I would be
very hesitant to either fail to ask their advice, or to ignore their words.

The writer of Proverbs declares, "Without wise leadership, a nation falls; with many counselors, there is safety" (Proverbs 11:14). I believe every one of us needs about three wise people to be a safety net as we walk the high wire of life. This might be a good time for you to make a list of the wise counselors in your life. How many do you have?

Seventh, *confess all sin to God and walk in obedience.* Too many people these days cringe at the word *obedience* while savoring the word *freedom.* But without obedience there can be no true freedom. Be obedient to God in the smallest details of your life, and thoroughly confess the sin that is revealed by the Spirit's conviction. Use Spiritual Breathing to confess and purify you throughout the day. Exhale by confessing your sins. Then inhale—receive by faith again the fullness and power of the Holy Spirit. This practice of Spiritual Breathing, if you are diligent about it, will radically transform your life.

Every time you undertake a significant effort for the Lord, you may experience difficult trials.

Eighth and finally, *expect the Holy Spirit to guide you as you take the next step by faith.* Our sovereign, omniscient Creator and Savior desires to guide us if we will only seek Him. Imagine you are driving through a crowded city. The most important appointment of your life is ahead, but traffic is heavy. You know this city fairly well, but who knows where today's tie-ups will be? Which route should you choose? Suddenly, with a smile, you turn on the radio. A helicopter pilot is giving traffic updates from the sky. You follow his advice and move easily toward your appointment.

The destination toward which we are moving in life is the only one that counts—sanctification. Every day we are moving closer to what God wants us to be, or we are becoming entangled in a confused world and its values. If we will only tune in to the "eye in the sky," the One who sees all and knows every step we should take, life will work infinitely better in every way.

Tune in every day to that frequency. Believe God's promise, "I will guide you along the best pathway for your life. I will advise you and watch over you" (Psalm 32:8).

That, my friend, is a promise to hold close to your heart.

Walking in the Spirit

Campus Crusade for Christ has reached many goals over half a century. But I assure you that we have encountered resistance on campus after campus, in city after city, and in country after country. Despite the constant conflicts, we have continued to serve the Lord as prayerfully, humbly, and as obediently as we have known how. Our ministry has had the privilege of working with tens of thousands of churches and thousands of mission groups of all denominations around the world. The ministry has been tremendously fruitful because we have stepped out in faith and allowed the Holy Spirit to guide us.

As you follow the Holy Spirit's leading and step out in faith, you, too, may encounter extraordinary opposition. This opposition may come from your old sin nature, the world, or Satan. Some believers think that when this happens, the Holy Spirit is not guiding them, or they assume God has closed a door. They wonder how they can know the difference. But the truth is that great blessings often follow great trials.

Every time you undertake a significant effort for the Lord, you may experience difficult trials. But if the Holy Spirit is leading you, you will invariably triumph regardless of the obstacles. God always blesses those who are obedient to Him, who desire to do His will, and who daily walk in His Holy Spirit. "We can make our plans, but the LORD determines our steps" (Proverbs 16:9). Trust and obey, for there is no other way.

This book's final section is about fruit—the kind that results from a life of walking in the Spirit. We will explore how to have a fruitful character, as well as a fruitful future.

Life Application

 Meditate on the Words of the Spirit. Take some time to memorize and meditate on the following verses:

■ "The LORD says, 'I will guide you along the best pathway for your life. I will advise you and watch over you'" (Psalm 32:8).

■ "If you need wisdom—if you want to know what God wants you to do—ask Him, and He will gladly tell you. He will not resent your asking. But when you ask Him, be sure that you really expect Him to answer, for a doubtful mind is as unsettled as a wave of the sea that is driven and tossed by the wind" (James 1:5,6).

 Focus on the Presence of the Spirit. Prayerfully answer these questions about your life:

■ In what areas of your life would you like to receive guidance from the Holy Spirit?

■ Have you experienced God's guidance in the past? What was the result?

■ Do you struggle with trusting God to know what is best for you? Why?

■ In what ways do you sometimes get in the way of the Holy Spirit's leading?

■ Where is the Holy Spirit leading you at present? How is He confirming it?

 Walk in the Power of the Spirit. Jesus is your Great Shepherd who wants to guide you to green pastures and walk with you through dark valleys. His Spirit, the Holy Spirit, lives within you. As you face decisions, commit yourself to following the Holy Spirit's leading by practicing the truths in the GUIDANCE acrostic:

Ground yourself in the truth of God's Word.

Use devotional time to listen to the Holy Spirit's leading.

Interpret Scripture passages, circumstances, and impressions carefully.

Decide to surrender your will to God continually.

Ask the Holy Spirit daily for wisdom and direction.

Note the counsel of godly advisors.

Confess all sin to God and walk in obedience.

Expect the Holy Spirit to guide you as you take the next step by faith.

Ask God to teach you to lean on the Spirit's guidance for every decision you make this week and for the rest of your life.

Part Three

A Transforming Presence

Chapter 13

Bearing Fruit in Character

F amily trees are fascinating. It is interesting to see how a man and woman, who lived perhaps two centuries ago, can have hundreds or even thousands of descendants in the modern world— or how another, once prolific family vanished from the earth. If a couple gives birth to seven or eight children who all have children of their own, within a few generations the family name is flourishing. We would call that a fruitful family line, like the one God promised to Abraham, Isaac, and Jacob.

We can bear fruit physically, but we can do so spiritually as well. You could draw a "family tree" of Campus Crusade for Christ International, and it would resemble that of a prolific family. We have over 70 ministries under the umbrella of this ministry and have helped start hundreds of other ministries to many groups such as students, executives, athletes, musicians, inner-city dwellers, and minorities. We have spawned ministries to couples and singles, to lawyers and doctors. Our work with the *JESUS* film, under the leadership of Paul Eshleman, has resulted in one of the most effective witnessing tools in modern Christian history. At this writing, over five billion people have been exposed to the gospel message through the *JESUS* film, with hundreds of millions responding. In other words, we feel the Spirit of God has led Campus Crusade to bear fruit in many diverse directions.

These principles of fruitfulness are also true, of course, on a personal level. The remaining chapters will discuss fruitfulness, and in this chapter we will explore the manner in which the Holy Spirit helps a believer bear fruit in character. I am often perplexed to see so many professing Christians, even those in full-time ministry, struggling to demonstrate the pleasing fruit that God expects us to produce. Many seemingly committed Christians are given to anger and impatience, while some lack joy or love for others. The character of Christ should be evident in converts we have won to Christ. But first of all, it should be manifest in the growth of godly character in our own lives.

When we use the word *fruit* in this context, we refer to the qualities that bring us to resemble Christ more and more as we abide in Him. He said, "I am the vine; you are the branches" (John 15:5). Have you ever looked closely at a grapevine? You will never see it struggling or straining to push out fruit. Fruit appears in season because the branches draw miraculous life from the vine. Given the right conditions—sunshine, water, and good soil—the grapevine produces abundant crops.

Love is the one fruit that guides and enhances the growth of the rest—the one that reigns supreme.

You need not struggle to be a fruitful believer, but simply abide in Christ. He is your sunshine from above, your living water, the rich soil in which you are planted. The Holy Spirit fills you as you abide in Him and obey Him. It is a matter of being *in* Christ rather than doing *for* Christ. My dear friend Charles Stanley writes, "The fruit of the Spirit was never intended to be a demonstration of our dedication and resolve. It is the evidence of our dependency on and sensitivity to the promptings of the Spirit."[1] In other words, you need not focus on love for this week, then patience for next week. Simply live each day in step with the Spirit, and He will bring a pleasing harvest of strong character qualities. You will be surprised and delighted to see patience, gentleness, and many other traits blooming in full flower in your life.

The more we walk in the power of the Holy Spirit and allow Him to guide and control our lives, the more Christ's character will shine in what we say and do. The Bible explains, "We will no longer be like children, forever changing our minds about what we believe because someone has told us something different or because someone has cleverly lied to us and made the lie sound like the truth. Instead, we will hold to the truth in love, becoming more and more in every way like Christ" (Ephesians 4:14,15).

When we begin to see bountiful fruit in the field of personal character, we will see, in particular, the greatest and most delicious fruit of them all—love.

Love Is Supreme

To begin looking at spiritual fruit, we turn naturally to the beloved list of spiritual character qualities that is found in Galatians. "When the Holy Spirit controls our lives, He will produce this kind of fruit in us: love, joy, peace, patience, kindness, goodness, faithfulness, gentleness, and self-control" (Galatians 5:22,23). Notice that in these verses you will find the word *and* rather than *or*. The Lord wants us to produce all of these characteristics in our lives, not just one or two. This is one of the beautiful qualities of abiding in Christ: we will show daily growth in love, daily growth in patience, daily growth in gentleness, and in all the rest. We may have one or more *gifts* of the Spirit, but we should demonstrate every *fruit* of the Spirit.

Notice the quality that Paul lists first. It is the one fruit that guides and enhances the growth of the rest—the one that reigns supreme. Elsewhere, Paul wrote that faith, hope, and love remain, but that "the greatest of these is love." He also wrote, "Let love be your highest goal" (1 Corinthians 13:13; 14:1).

Love is the ultimate test of our authenticity as God's children. Jesus said, "Your love for one another will prove to the world that you are My disciples" (John 13:35). Without love, we can do nothing for God. In 1 Corinthians 13, Paul cites the many wonderful traits of true, godly love. Its essence is sacrifice—giving unselfishly of ourselves—and we can accomplish that highest goal only by abiding in Christ through the enabling of the Holy Spirit. The Bible uses the Greek word *agape* for this highest and noblest form of love. It can only be imparted to us by the Holy Spirit because it is supernatural. He helps us to love others by His power.

Agape love is based on choice—an act of the will—not on feelings or circumstances. We can all love those who love us in return. But it takes the power of the Holy Spirit to help us unconditionally love our enemies, to pray for them, to go the extra mile, and to turn the other cheek. Jesus demonstrated this unconditional love when He died on the cross—not just for us but for the very men who despised and persecuted Him. Such a love turns the world and its conventions upside down. It can be explained no other way but through the power and majesty of Christ, pouring Himself into human hearts through the Holy Spirit.

Initially you meet Christ, then you slowly come to know Him more deeply. In time, I pray that you will learn to actually *abide* in Him. We will say more about this toward the end of this chapter. For now let us emphasize that as you come to know Christ more fully, it is inevitable that His love will begin to show in your life. And to know Him is to manifest His love. He is our ideal in all things, but this one wonderful word, *love*, captures His meaning better than any other. Love is the theme, as the old chorus tells us; love is supreme.

You will grow to love your neighbor as God loves him. You will learn to love God more deeply, and even to love yourself as God loves you. As love becomes the theme of your life, you will naturally find more *joy* than you have ever experienced. You will find in love the *peace* that passes all understanding. Because of love it will be possible for you to be *patient*—and so on. The fruit of the Spirit will grow through abiding in the vine, and all of that delicious fruit will also bear the taste of the greatest of them all—love.

Joy, Peace, and Patience

The prophet Nehemiah declared, "The joy of the LORD is your strength!" (Nehemiah 8:10). Such a joy can come only from the Holy Spirit.

Do you remember the joy of your first love? True, powerful love is a joyous thing. But the joy of the Spirit is more powerful and significant than what the world considers to be joy. The joy of the Lord is deep, abiding, and based on truth rather than emotions. It runs deeper than mere happiness because it never rests on fleeting circumstances. Our joy comes directly from God and from the permanent truth of what He has done for us. Jesus Christ has pardoned us from all our sins, great and small. He has freed us from guilt along with the awful toll it takes on human relationships. He abides with us intimately on a daily basis. And when this life is finished, He promises us an eternal life with Him more wonderful than we can imagine. How could we not feel joy in harboring those truths in our hearts? To abide in Christ means to have them always before you, and that will bring you joy.

Do you believe there is a joy that transcends circumstances—even tragic ones? Dr. R. A. Torrey, who founded the Bible Institute of Los Angeles (BIOLA University), endured a period of terrible grief when his 12-year-old daughter was killed in an accident. Even though Dr. and Mrs. Torrey knew their beloved Elisabeth had gone to be with the Lord, they were brokenhearted as they faced the lonely years ahead without her presence.

In his grief Dr. Torrey cried out to the Lord for help. Then the power of the Holy Spirit broke through the misery in his heart. Dr. Torrey described the feeling as something like a fountain of eternal joy welling up within him. No matter how much he mourned his daughter, the joy of the Lord was the most compelling force within him—a fountain springing up, even amidst tragedy, to eternal life.[2] The joy of the Lord is no small thing—it is unstoppable, and ultimately more powerful than even the hurts of life. Jesus said, "Yes, your joy will overflow!" (John 15:11). It is a joy the world cannot take away, and it will well up within you as you grow in Christ.

Along with his joy, Dr. Torrey felt *peace*. Jesus promised His disciples, "I am leaving you with a gift—peace of mind and heart. And the peace I give isn't like the peace the world gives. So don't be troubled or afraid" (John 14:27). In times of terrible anxiety, your character can come to manifest not only joy but a peace that transcends present difficulties.

Why does such a peace grow within us? It is because we are no longer at war with God. Your sins have been forgiven and, through the Spirit, you can abide in His presence. You may still live in a difficult world, but when you encounter terrible circumstances that pass all understanding, you meet them with a peace that passes all understanding. The world has nothing to offer in such times. But as Christians we understand why someone like Corrie ten Boom, placed in a World War II prison camp, could actually *love* her persecutors, feel true *joy* while those around her were embittered, and be filled with a *peace* that undermined the tormentors who wanted to break her character. Their fruit was bitter, but hers was eternal; it was the fruit of a character built through abiding in Christ.

Patience, Kindness, and Goodness

As the Spirit molds you in love, in joy, and in peace, He will be teaching you the virtue of *patience*. "Patient endurance is what you need now, so you will continue to do God's will. Then you will receive all that He has promised" (Hebrews 10:36).

Patience, also known in the Word as *longsuffering*, comes from a Greek term that describes our ability to endure evil without returning it. This is not something that comes naturally to any human being. Like love, it goes against the grain of our corrupt human nature. It points directly to the wisdom and perfect love of the Spirit who acts in love rather than reacting in anger. Patience allows us to accept what comes to us not only from others but from life itself. We wait for the right person to marry. We wait for the career opportunity that never seems to come. We wait to have a child, even as the years fade away. Why would we not give in to frustration and impatience? We are steadfast because the Spirit counsels wisdom. He teaches us to trust in God's divine timing.

The Christian knows that time and destiny are in the hands of a God who loves us. His plan for us is perfect, and it ultimately makes no sense for us to lash out in frustration when we cannot see the details of the schedule. Paul wrote, "Be glad for all God is planning for you. Be patient in trouble, and always be prayerful" (Romans 12:12).

Along with love, it is patience that expresses itself in that fruit of the Spirit called *kindness*. Again, patience restrains us from striking back. "Be kind to each other, tenderhearted, forgiving one another, just as God through Christ has forgiven you" (Ephesians 4:32). Kindness might be described as a sweetness of character, and it holds a quiet power that takes the world by surprise. This kind person is rarely at the center of any great commotion. A kind man never performs his acts of righteousness for public praise. A kind woman reaches out to those who are lonely and ignored, just as Jesus did. Kindness is love behind the scenes, love broken down into small but meaningful gestures. The world grows more and more unkind, but the believer grows in compassion each day as he becomes more like Christ.

Booker T. Washington tells the story of his older brother's kindness to him. The shirts worn by the slaves on the plantation were made of flax, a very inexpensive fiber. When Booker was a young boy, the course fibers of the shirt were so rough and abrasive to his tender skin that he had difficulty wearing them. To alleviate his suffering, Booker's older brother wore the shirts until they were broken in and no longer irritated his brother's skin.[3]

Kindness is related to still another fruit, the one we call *goodness.* Perhaps this one needs a bit of explanation. To be good, by definition, is to be like God. Goodness is ruled by higher standards of righteousness, and it opposes evil. "For though your hearts were once full of darkness, now you are full of light from the Lord, and your behavior should show it! For this light within you produces only what is good and right and true" (Ephesians 5:8,9).

The Christian knows that time and destiny are in the hands of a God who loves us. His plan for us is perfect.

Goodness is not a passive thing, but a very active one. Goodness is the love of God expressed in our actions. Just as the light rushes through to abolish the darkness, so goodness moves through the world and works in the name of the Lord, accomplishing the purposes that matter to Him.

Can you see the reasoning behind the order in which the fruit is listed, beginning with the supremacy of love? Love is joyful; joy breaks through and brings peace. Those at peace can be patient, and patience makes kindness possible. Kindness, in turn, is an expression of goodness. These fruit all grow together and lend their unique flavors to one another. As we understand this sequence, we begin to form a picture of the kind of life the Spirit makes possible for us—and an inspiring, attractive picture it is.

Faithfulness, Gentleness, and Self-Control

As we have seen, the character traits nurtured by God's Spirit are closely aligned to one another. Someone who is patient, kind, and good is also likely to be *faithful*.

Jesus counseled a church, "Remain faithful even when facing death, and I will give you the crown of life" (Revelation 2:10). If we want to offer the ultimate test of character, perhaps it would be the test of faithfulness. Among early believers, some were drawn to Christ only to scatter in fear at the first sign of persecution. But those who abided deeply in Christ showed a faith that could endure, even in the face of death. The reward for that, as Jesus tells us in Revelation, is "the crown of life." There are rewards in both this world and the next. Faithfulness implies truthfulness, sincerity, and trust. It inspires confidence and greatness in others. Hebrews chapter 11 glories in the faithfulness of Abraham, Sarah, Moses, Jacob, Rahab, David, Samuel, the prophets, and numerous others who go unnamed.

Over and over in the Scriptures, our Lord calls us to be faithful. Someday you and I will stand before Jesus Christ and give an account of our lives. We will be judged not by our success, achievements, or performance—but by our faithfulness to Him. My greatest desire is to stand before Jesus and receive the crown of life. I want to hear Him say, "Well done, my good and faithful servant. You have been faithful in handling this small amount, so now I will give you many more responsibilities. Let's celebrate together!" (Matthew 25:21).

Faithfulness is stirring, but what about *gentleness*? We often make the mistake of assigning to it the idea of being passive, timid, and ineffectual. But Jesus seems to promise tremendous rewards to the gentle. He said, "God blesses those who are gentle and lowly, for the whole earth will belong to them" (Matthew 5:5). Gentleness has nothing to do with weakness. On the contrary, it is quiet strength under great control—for this is the precise meaning of the term as it is used in the Scriptures. Can you think of any better model of that concept than Jesus Himself? He was gentle but never passive, never weak, never ineffectual. Children flocked to Him, yet centurions and tax collectors were interested in His words. He was both tough and tender in a way that the Spirit enables us to be as well.

Gentleness is like taming a stallion or calming the raging waters. It is not for the weak. The gentle person can control his tongue and his impulses. And quite naturally this brings us to our final fruit of godly character—*self-control*. We might think of this fruit as the final victory of love over our old sinful, rebellious, carnal human nature. How seldom we see it in today's world of personal self-gratification. "It is better to be patient than powerful; it is better to have self-control than to conquer a city" (Proverbs 16:32). Indeed, it is easier to conquer a city than to conquer one's own impulses.

The biblical term for self-control carries the meaning of strength that enables us to master our thoughts, our emotions, and our deeds. The Spirit takes every thought captive for Christ, but also our feelings and the works of our hands. Life apart from God is a life out of control, but the Spirit gradually focuses us, with ever sharper precision, on the purposes of Christ in this world. We are self-controlled because our mission is too great to waste a moment on trivial matters. When we reach that mindset, we experience the victory that God wants us to have. We become men and women of character, and we bear more than a passing resemblance to Christ Himself. That is a breathtaking thought—but it is the will of God for you, and it is very attainable.

Tending Your Garden of Godly Character

As we consider these wonderful character traits that are embodied as the fruit of the Spirit, we naturally think of Christians we know who model them so well. I think of close friends and spiritual leaders I have admired. What seems obvious is that anyone who has demonstrated *one* of these qualities has demonstrated all of them in varying degrees—that is how the Spirit works. He is interested in developing in our lives the fruits of love, joy, peace, patience, and all the rest.

I have one other observation about those who excel in godly character. We must realize that they are not necessarily the "Super Christians" who have achieved fame and recognition. Our leading pastors, teachers, evangelists, and others have cultivated the *gifts* of the Spirit, but it is another matter entirely to cultivate the *fruit* of the Spirit. You and I can think of old friends, Sunday school teachers, co-workers, and relatives of shining character. They may be obscure to the world, but I can assure you that the angels hold them in high esteem. The believers have cultivated the fruit of Christian character.

Jesus said that trees and people can both be identified by their fruit (Matthew 7:20). Have you ever walked through a fruit market and evaluated the produce? We squeeze the melons lightly, examine the shine on the apples, and inspect the size of the oranges and lemons. Think of your life as an open market, with the public walking by to see what kind of fruit you produce. Will they buy it? Perhaps they would find that the grapes of patience are too puny, or the apples of joy are a bit spoiled. You would like your fruit to be the best it can be. So how do you cultivate it?

First, give some attention to the soil. If you have ever done any gardening, you know how crucial it is to plant your seeds in healthy soil. Not just any dirt will do! For healthy spiritual growth, we must ground ourselves in the good soil of the Word of God. Reading the Bible daily is only the beginning. We must be *planted* in the Word, absorbing it and allowing the Spirit to transform our hearts and minds. David the shepherd thought in these same botanical terms when he wrote these verses:

> His delight is in the law of the LORD, and on His law he meditates day and night. He is like a tree planted by streams of water, which yields its fruit in season and whose leaf does not wither. Whatever he does prospers (Psalm 1:2,3, NIV).

Earnestly study God's Word. Then, watch out for the weeds. If you have ever visited a large, well-tended, public garden, you have known a special joy. Buchard Gardens in Western Canada covers acres of land. It is filled with every flower imaginable, carefully tended to bloom at the pinnacle of perfection. It also boasts perfectly clipped hedges and lawns as well as meandering paths and twining vines. But if this lovely garden were left untended for long, weeds would quickly encroach upon it, crowding out the lovely flowers, spoiling the lawns, and ruining the view.

Our weeds, of course, are the sins that try to creep into our lives at all times. We should keep short accounts with God, confessing and repenting, practicing Spiritual Breathing as regularly as a skilled gardener deftly uproots weeds in his garden. Take extra time for prayer to ask the Spirit to reveal any unknown sin in your life. The Bible assures us, "If we confess our sins to Him, He is faithful and just to forgive us and to cleanse us from every wrong" (1 John 1:9). Sin, if unattended, will surround the fruit of godly character and choke it out. We must not let that happen.

Our Food and Water

Thriving plants must be watered and fed regularly as well. Neglect is deadly. If plants are not watered and fertilized regularly, they develop bugs, mold, fungus, and disease. In the garden of character, we meet with God in our daily prayer in order to be refreshed by the Holy Spirit. We also need to be committed to a local body of believers who can encourage and strengthen us in our walk. The writer of Hebrews proclaimed, "Let us not neglect our meeting together, as some people do, but encourage and warn each other, especially now that the day of His coming back again is drawing near" (10:25).

Sunlight, too, is a crucial consideration. Have you ever tried to grow houseplants in a closet? Of course not. Living things need light, and so do we. The Light of life is the Spirit of Christ within us. Jesus described Himself as "the light that leads to life" (John 8:12). We are commanded to be filled with the Spirit, for only then can we grow and produce fruit. This is a very dark world in which we live, and it is no wonder that strong character is a rare commodity. There is a shortage of trust, for there is a shortage of integrity. But the Spirit illuminates your soul so that there is always the bright sunshine of springtime within you. No matter what difficulties may confront you in life, your character draws its life from the Spirit as it grows toward maturity.

Then there is the interesting matter of pruning. Most plants actually produce far more flowers and fruit when they are pruned, for pruning focuses and redirects growth. It eliminates wildness and disorganization. Wisteria is an excellent example. In the fall, the vine sends out runners in all directions. Let the runners grow and you will have a fine leafy vine the next spring. But if you clip the runners, an abundance of fragrant flowers will be produced.

Jesus said, "I am the true vine, and my Father is the gardener. He cuts off every branch that doesn't produce fruit, and He prunes the branches that do bear fruit so they will produce even more" (John 15:1,2). Pruning can be painful and discouraging, but if we want to produce abundant fruit for the Lord, we must undergo discipline. We must withstand trials to pass the test. As all good earthly parents know, loving discipline and the lessons from life are necessary to produce mature children. So it is with God's children.

Pruning can be painful, but if we want to produce abundant fruit for the Lord, we must undergo discipline.

Growth, of course, requires time. Just as plants must bloom in season, there are no shortcuts to a godly character. The fruit of the Spirit grows slowly, so do not become discouraged if you do not see results right away. Invite God to begin transforming you, and submit to His work on His schedule.

Abiding in the True Vine

All the while, as we are patient, we remember that we are attached to Christ Himself. This is what Jesus meant when He said, "I am the vine; you are the branches" (John 15:5). The thinnest, weakest branches are ripped away during a storm. Then they become firewood, or they die in the dust. But as you grow in the Spirit, you will never be torn away. Jesus has promised that no one could snatch us away (John 10:28, 29). Meanwhile, abide in Him. This means to dwell with Him in the deepest possible intimacy.

When you first met your best friend, you probably did not spend much time together. Nor was your conversation particularly open or candid. But in time, as you came to love one another, your time together increased in quantity and quality—you abided together and built a strong relationship that no storm would destroy. This is the way of abiding in Christ, too. Jesus tells us in John 15:4,5 that if we remain rooted deeply in Him, we will bear much fruit. How could we do otherwise? If you want to cultivate the most godly character, the only way to do so is to be deeply connected to the One you long to resemble—Jesus Christ Himself. Consider His character:

- He was so loving that He reached out to minister to people He passed.

- He was so joyful that He attended parties and celebrated when sinners found God.

- He was so peaceful that He calmed stormy waters.

- He was so patient that He never gave up on immature, quarreling disciples.

- He was so kind that He embraced lepers.

- He was so good that He cared for the physical hunger of a large crowd.

- He was so faithful that He never neglected prayer, even when His time was short.

- He was so gentle that children rushed to Him everywhere He traveled.

- He was so self-controlled that He took our punishment when He could have escaped.

Jesus shined most brightly when He faced His most terrible moments. That is the greatest miracle of godly character, which produces shining perfection when pressure is applied. Over time, the darkest coal, under tremendous heat and pressure, can produce the most beautiful diamond. In the same way, your character can be transformed to be like Christ. All you need to do is stay rooted in Christ and abide in Him. Then invite the Holy Spirit to take the lead as you plant yourself in the grounding of His inspired Word, remove the weeds of sin, bask in the living water of deep, abiding prayer, and submit to the necessary pruning of spiritual discipline. Tend the garden of your character in this way, my friend, and I assure you that you will grow a godly character.

Then, do you know what happens next? Others will see the garden of your character and be inspired to tend their own. If enough of us abide in Christ and live this way, be assured that the darkness will begin to subside here and there, and the world may come to resemble—just a bit—that beautiful and perfect garden in which Adam and Eve began life.

Once you are filled with the Spirit, and are bearing the fruit of character, how should you live from this day forward? That is the topic of our next chapter.

Life Application

 Meditate on the Words of the Spirit. Make it a priority to memorize and meditate on the following verses:

- "The way to identify a tree or a person is by the kind of fruit that is produced" (Matthew 7:20).

- "When the Holy Spirit controls our lives, He will produce this kind of fruit in us: love, joy, peace, patience, kindness, goodness, faithfulness, gentleness, and self-control" (Galatians 5:22,23).

 Focus on the Presence of the Spirit. Search your heart as you ask the following questions:

- What personal attitudes stand in the way of your bearing fruit in character?

- In what ways has your character grown since you have become a believer?

- Which of the fruit of the Spirit is most lacking in your life? Why?

- Is it more important to do more good works or to become more Christ like? Why?

 Walk in the Power of the Spirit. The Holy Spirit longs to produce His fruit in you. Ask God to produce the fruit of the Spirit in you by praying the following:

Gracious Father, I ask You to produce Your fruit—the fruit of Your character—in my life. I commit myself to spend time in Your Word to know You better and to cultivate Your truth in my heart and mind. I confess all of my sins to You.

Thank You for Your abundant, merciful forgiveness. May Your Spirit quickly convict me of any sins so that nothing may damage my relationship with You. I commit myself to a prayer life of adoration, praise, thanksgiving, and petitions.

I commit myself also to a local body of believers who will challenge me to mature, a place where I can use my gifts to help build that body.

I desire to be a godly person. I surrender my life to Jesus Christ, my Lord. Fill me completely with Your Holy Spirit, O Lord. I freely give myself to You for service and growth. Thank You for Your goodness and love.

May I always abide in the vine, which is Christ, bearing much fruit in the power of Your Holy Spirit. In Christ's glorious name. Amen.

Chapter 14

Bearing Fruit
for a Lifetime

H e was a warrior of towering reputation, and his enemies feared him greatly. More than anything else, they feared his sword, whose power had inspired wild rumors and legends. After hearing enough of these wild tales, his king finally demanded an examination of the notorious battle weapon. The warrior had his celebrated sword delivered to the palace by special messenger.

The king examined the weapon closely before finally sending back this message: "I see nothing wonderful in the sword; I cannot understand why any man should be afraid of it."

The warrior must have smiled as he read the king's words, for he replied, "Your Majesty has been pleased to examine the sword, but I did not send the arm that wielded it. If you had examined that, you would have understood the mystery."[1]

None of us, in our own strength, is any more impressive than that sword. But as we submit to the Holy Spirit and allow Him to wield us in the power of God, we become amazing instruments for God's glory. We can do all things through Christ who strengthens us.

The Spirit is God's powerful presence within us, and He makes all the difference in life. In this book we have outlined the way He teaches us truth, guides our prayer, motivates us to holiness, and many other amazing purposes He will fulfill. I pray we have sufficiently introduced the essential and practical truths of His mission and ministry. But it seems more obvious than ever that no book about the Holy Spirit could tell His full story or cover any measure of His greatness. The power and purposes of the Comforter are infinite and far too deep for our understanding. All we can do is marvel at the news that the Spirit of God is pleased to dwell within us in all His fullness and to make us instruments of His will.

Next to our Lord's crucifixion and resurrection, I believe the arrival of the Spirit at Pentecost was the most earth-shaking event in human history. As the Spirit arrived to transform the followers of Jesus, they in turn became transformers. The cowardly became the courageous, and the defeated became victorious and dynamic. Soon the news of the gospel was penetrating every nation, every cultural barrier, and the Roman Empire itself was unable to withstand the Spirit's mighty momentum.

Best of all, I can tell you that the Holy Spirit is still alive, well, and turning millions of lives upside down today. It remains only for us to follow His lead. If we do, we will surely duplicate or surpass the achievements of the first-century believers. But we cannot lag behind the mighty purposes of God. Paul admonishes us, "Since we live by the Spirit, let us keep in step with the Spirit" (Galatians 5:25, NIV). This verse paints a picture of moving with purpose, walking with determination toward a goal. This is the picture I wish for us to fix in our minds as we finish the journey of this book. I pray that you will think of your future as a long and exciting track, leading you to higher ground with every step, and finally to the finish line and a crown of life from the hand of the Master Himself.

I can tell you that the Holy Spirit is still alive, well, and turning millions of lives upside down today.

Walk in the Spirit, keep in step, and He will plant your feet on higher ground. That is your future. Let us take a glimpse of what it holds for you.

Keeping in Step

Walking in the Spirit means walking in faith. Life has many twists and turns, and at times you will move through darkness where the footing is treacherous. But your hand will be in His, and like a little child you will learn to depend totally upon the One whose step never wavers. Keep in step with the Spirit and you will learn total dependence upon our Great God and Savior.

Then, as your faith and dependence grow, you will find yourself taking greater and bolder steps into the unknown. No more "baby steps" for you—you will want to take great, heroic strides for the Lord. That means attempting goals in His name that are so outrageous and humanly impossible that without His supernatural power, they are bound to fail. The finest Christian leaders I have known fit that profile. So great is their faith that they never hesitate when they hear the word *impossible*. They know that those are the occasions in which the name of the Lord is most glorified. When we take on seemingly insurmountable obstacles and tasks for our Lord with the help of the Holy Spirit and we succeed, great glory will be given to our great Lord.

God's name was glorified when Abraham and Sarah trusted Him for a child, even though Sarah was ninety years old. He was glorified when Moses led the Israelites to freedom, even with the great army of the Pharaoh in hot pursuit. He was glorified when David overcame a giant no one else had the courage to face; when Daniel was steadfast even in a lions' den; when Peter and Paul defied Roman emperors and murderous crowds. His name was found worthy of praise when Hudson Taylor broke through into Inland China, when Billy Graham won millions of converts at his crusades, and when Explo '74 turned South Korea upside down for Christ. The Spirit has never stopped moving forward, and He is waiting for us to fall in step. On that day, you too can overcome the impossible because you are willing to be obedient and confident in the power of the Spirit in your life.

The Spirit of God will not limit Himself because you are currently single or raising a family or working in the business world or pursuing an education. The precise circumstances of your life are only the background; His power is what matters, and it is not reserved for pastors or far-away missionaries. As a matter of fact, it may be that God is glorified the most when a custodian, a school teacher, a plumber, or a homemaker does mighty things for Him. I need not know the details of your background to tell you that the Spirit is ready to use you in some way right now. The question is, are you willing to be used?

The fact is that even if you try as hard as you can, you cannot imagine the magnificence of what God can and will do through you. "Now glory be to God who by His mighty power at work within us is able to do far more than we would ever dare to ask or even dream of —infinitely beyond our highest prayers, desires, thoughts, or hopes" (Ephesians 3:20, TLB). His purposes are wider than our dreams, dearer than our hopes.

But what if you are afraid? The Spirit gives courage the world cannot explain.

What if you are afraid of falling into sin? The Spirit will strengthen you beyond its control, if you let Him. "Now, the Lord is the Spirit, and wherever the Spirit of the Lord is, He gives freedom" (2 Corinthians 3:17).

If you desire to live a life free of fear and the devastation of sin and rebellion, walk in the power of the Holy Spirit. He is eager to help you.

Overpowering in Praise

Keep in step with the Spirit, and your life will be filled with praise and worship, not fear and failure. The Spirit will take you places you never would have dreamed, and give you victories beyond your hopes. You will be constantly focused on those great purposes that glorify God. You will be using your gifts and enjoying the satisfaction of doing the things that God made you to do. You will be bearing incredible fruit in the attitudes of love, joy, peace, and so on. Your relationships will be edifying and positive.

Yet there will be wonderful surprises all along the way. You will not be some kind of mindless robot mechanically carrying out assigned tasks. You will be no cog in a heavenly machine, but the living, breathing, feeling person you were always meant to be, coming into your own because you are one of God's own, fully surrendered to Him and to His kingdom. You will clearly see that any other kind of life is no more than a shadow of living, filled with spiritual confusion and divided loyalties. Only as you keep in step with the Spirit will you see how life was meant to be lived, and only then does the world have any hope of reconciliation with God.

Life in the Spirit is filled with joy, and it is typified by music. "Let the Holy Spirit fill and control you. Then you will sing psalms and hymns and spiritual songs among yourselves, making music to the Lord in your hearts. And you will always give thanks for everything to God the Father in the name of our Lord Jesus Christ" (Ephesians 5:18–20). Does that sound like the quality of life you would like to have? It brings the Spirit great joy to fill you with great joy.

Here is one example of that kind of life. When Jehoshaphat was king in Judah, a great multitude of his enemies came against him to destroy him. The king and the people were terrified, and they rushed to the temple to seek God's face through prayer and fasting. They asked Him what they should do. God told the king that He, the Lord Himself, would fight for Judah. If God was for them, who could be against them? The joyful king led all the people in a time of worship. And he had a wonderful surprise in store.

The next day, the enemies of Judah must have been struck speechless when they saw the approaching people of God. The army of Judah was coming, of course, but in front of them came marching the choir, a delegation making music for all it was worth. God's people knew the battle would go to the Lord, and the proper response was to go out singing, praising, and worshiping Him. But the army of Judah had even less to do than they expected. "At the moment they began to sing and give praise, the LORD caused the armies of Ammon, Moab, and Mount Seir to start fighting among themselves. The armies of Moab and Ammon turned against their allies from Mount Seir and killed every one of them. After they had finished off the army of Seir, they turned on each other" (2 Chronicles 20:22,23). In the face of God's power, the worst of the world will self-destruct as the name of God is glorified. We go out in worship for we know the victory is already ours.

The Bible tells us that God inhabits the praises of His people—that He actually makes His throne within our praise and worship: "But You are holy, who inhabit the praises of Israel" (Psalm 22:3, NKJ). I find that to be an exciting thought. As Jehoshaphat's armies moved forward, they sang praises to God, and He was among them. Praise God in all that you do, and His Spirit will embrace and empower you in a special way, from the throne He establishes within your praises.

Overcoming in Faith

It would be wrong to give the impression that you will never encounter strife or hardship as you walk in the Spirit. As you keep in step and move forward in praise, you will still come up against terrible strongholds. You will face opposition, even in the form of other believers. You may experience doubts over what the Spirit has led you to do. As long as you keep your eyes on our great God and Savior, and stay in perfect communion with the Spirit, you will not stumble.

I have experienced these challenges again and again. In the early 1970s, God impressed upon me to build an international leadership university. With the encouragement of the mayor, we miraculously purchased 5,000 acres of land in La Jolla, California, and we succeeded in doing so without relying upon any Campus Crusade for Christ finances. The large acreage was for the purpose of building Life Estate homes to endow the University. But we soon encountered obstacles, including zoning problems and a new mayor who was dead set against the development of that land for a Christian university.

We prayed, sought God's confirmation, and spent hours meeting with the zoning committee, mayor, and city council. But there was no progress. It could have been very easy to doubt that this was the will of God for us after all. As years passed and the battle dragged on, some Christians turned against the project. They complained about me and even called me names. I was accused of using the Lord's money unwisely. This was a time of great personal testing for me. Yet I can assure you that God never let me have one moment of disquiet or lose one moment of sleep over this conflict. In fact, I now know that our plans were delayed because God was preparing something better.

Even as we were suffering through the long agonizing wait, wondering what God was up to, the amazing video and Internet technologies were quietly emerging. Instead of building a campus, which would have cost hundreds of millions of dollars, we can now teach countless people around the world on the Internet through our own form of distance learning. The Internet university we are developing is much larger and more far-reaching than anything I could have imagined. We were thinking in terms of bricks, mortar, and a zip code. But the Spirit of God had a vision that embraced the world and transcended geography. Thankfully, the Holy Spirit enabled me to trust God and allow His peace to comfort me during this time of testing.

I would counsel you to keep your eyes on Jesus during such times of stress. I have a simple system for doing that: love God with all your heart, soul, mind, and strength. Meditate on the Word of God, obey His commands, trust His promises, and examine the lives of the men and women of faith who have gone before us. Those saints did two things when they faced hard times. First, they maintained their faith by insisting on viewing their circumstances from an eternal perspective. Instead of being overwhelmed by their current situation, they relied on the Lord's everlasting promises. Second, they did not concern themselves with repercussions from nonbelievers when they followed the Lord. They trusted God to take care of the fallout.

I now know that our plans were delayed because God was preparing something even better.

I am not a prophet, and I cannot predict what your own tests and trials will be. But if you lay the groundwork of keeping in step with the Holy Spirit now, all you need to do is keep walking, keep watching Him, and by faith put one foot in front of the other. If you do, He will never allow you to stumble.

Overflowing in Witness

One other thing will happen when you keep in step with the Spirit: you will hear other steps coming behind you.

Have you noticed what happens to someone who seems to know where he is going and what he is doing? People begin to follow him; he becomes a leader without even realizing it. But this principle is infinitely more true of a believer who lives and walks in the Spirit. His or her life will be attractive. It will showcase the use of gifts and the presence of character, those two great visible effects of the Spirit's presence. Sharing Christ will no longer be a chore, and you will find that you no longer need to start the conversation quite so often. People will come to you, and they will have plenty of questions. They will

209

approach you in their own times of confusion, or simply out of curiosity to know more about what makes you what you are. They will sense that nothing on earth can explain the radiance and joy they see in a Spirit-filled life.

Nothing captures the attention of the world so much as *quiet* power. For some believers, witnessing is a real burden and a subject of fear. But when those same people are filled with the Spirit, when they keep in step with Him, when they march into battle with a song of praise on their lips—and when this victorious march becomes a lifestyle—then the fear evaporates to be replaced by joy. We cannot wait to tell others about Christ, for we remember what life used to be like when we lived according to our own plans. We can remember what it means to struggle through life without the answers. And we know that the day we received Christ and began to grow in Him, the miracle began.

A picture is worth a thousand words, and the picture of a life in step with the Spirit speaks volumes.

In the joy of the Holy Spirit, we will want to be proactive in going to people and telling them about Christ, because it is necessary in order to bring them to a moment of decision. But well before that moment, we will already have told them many things without ever speaking. It is said that a picture is worth a thousand words, and the picture of a life in step with the Spirit speaks volumes —or rather, it sings choruses. People can hear the beautiful music of a Spirit-filled life through the ears of their soul, for God has placed within them a great longing to come home to Him. They will recognize in your life the distant melody of that land and that life they long for, and they will come up beside you to ask where you are going. A conversation about Christ will ensue. And before you know it, they too will be following the Lord. This is very much how Jesus called His disciples, as they left all that they had to follow Him.

You, my friend, will become a spiritual Pied Piper. People will hear the music of God's kingdom as you march toward the promised land, and the melody will be irresistible. They will fall into step with you, and others, in turn, will begin to follow *them*. Perhaps, in time, you will raise an army—and you will know that the Lord will go with you. That is the victorious march of keeping in step with the Spirit.

Owning the Crown of Victory

So we walk in the Spirit, we keep in step, but where does the road lead?

It leads, in the end, to the only destination worth setting out for. The Spirit will take us home into the arms of a loving Father. Can you imagine the joy and the celebration of that arrival? If you have ever seen the running of a marathon race—a tradition that extends back into Bible times—you know that there are long, weary miles followed by tumultuous applause as the runners enter the stadium. The final lap is the easiest one to run, for the battle has been fought. The runners have endured. Their feet have not failed.

I believe that when you and I enter the great assembly in heaven and take that victory lap, there will be the cheering and songs of praise from the angels, who will all be gathered with the saints who have gone before us. But we will join in the music, for it will be directed toward God, not us. And as we come to the great throne that sits in the center of that assembly, we will gain our reward. Paul, James, John, and Peter all tell us that there is a crown given to believers when we finally come to stand before our Lord. Here is how Paul describes the glorious finish in what must be close to the final message we have from the apostle:

> I have fought a good fight, I have finished the race, and I have remained faithful. And now the prize awaits me—the crown of righteousness that the Lord, the righteous Judge, will give me on that great day of His return. And the prize is not just for me but for all who eagerly look forward to His glorious return (2 Timothy 4:7,8).

I know how Paul felt, because I experience all the deep emotions he expressed in that letter to Timothy. I am near the end of my race, and my heart and mind are filled with praise to our mighty Savior who has brought me so far. I can only wonder where I would be today if I had not asked Him be my Savior and Lord. I wonder what my life would be like if I had not discovered the incredible presence, peace, and power of the Holy Spirit of God. It has been a long journey, and one not without its bends and bumps in the road. But I would not trade a moment of it for all the world, for I know where this road leads. It leads to a glorious place called heaven. The Bible says, "No eye has seen, no ear has heard, and no mind has imagined what God has prepared for those who love him" (1 Corinthians 2:9).

Now I look back at those who run a few steps behind me. I exhort you to run the race with the wind of the Spirit as your breath, with the fire of the Spirit as your energy, with the living water of Christ as your sustenance. Let Him fill you. Let Him give you the power to keep moving forward without giving in to fear, weariness, or fatigue. Keep your eyes on the prize, though that final destination may lay far distant in years or around the next corner.

Into the Victor's Circle

Decide today that you will live in the joy and victory of the resurrection through the enabling of the Holy Spirit. Trust in Him. You will walk, then you will run, and perhaps you will even fly: "But those who wait on the LORD will find new strength. They will fly high on wings like eagles. They will run and not grow weary. They will walk and not faint" (Isaiah 40:31).

Life will be exciting as today's halting, stumbling steps become, day by day, more like the blessed feet of Jesus Himself. You will have a goal and a destination, and all the aspects of your life—your work, your relationships, your time—will find their proper place.

It will remain only for you to stay in the race, and run to win. Again, Paul tells us: "All athletes practice strict self-control. They do it to win a prize that will fade away, but we do it for an eternal prize. So I run straight to the goal with purpose in every step. I am not like a boxer who misses his punches" (1 Corinthians 9:25,26). *Yes, purpose in every step.* Does that not sound like the kind of life you would like to have now and forever?

Run to win. Run for the crown. And visualize yourself with that great, gleaming arena finally looming before you, at the end of all your years. Listen! All the heavenly host can be heard within the arena as your strong, disciplined feet draw closer to the entrance. Then you are inside, and there is beautiful pandemonium—the voices of innumerable angels, and the applause of all those believers who have arrived before you.

As you finally come to the center of the arena, a victor's crown is set upon your head. You look up into those eyes—those eyes of love, holiness, and perfection, and that glance you could not have met before today. And you see His smile. It is not as if that wonderful face is unfamiliar to you, because you recognize it as the face of the greatest Friend you have had these many years. It is the smile of that Friend who has whispered in your ear at every turn, who has empowered you at every conflict, who has built character within you at every opportunity. This is the Friend who was the giver of the gifts that defined your life and service. He is the One who came alongside you one wonderful day and never departed. He is the One who made life worth living, and turned every other relationship into a masterpiece of its own.

He has been your Friend, but now He stands revealed as the Alpha and the Omega, the Creator and King. He speaks: "Well done, good and faithful servant." And He places upon your head the crown of victory, the one you were promised and which marks you as one who followed to the end.

What can you do then? Only fall upon your knees. Only weep in joy and gratitude. Only reach up with trembling hands to remove the gleaming crown, and to place it at the feet of the One who bestowed it.

Then I believe He will smile with a light that could illuminate infinite galaxies, and He will say, one more time, "Well done!" And you will enjoy the fellowship that is your true reward, the eternal and perfect presence of our wonderful Lord.

Life Application

 Meditate on the Words of the Spirit. Memorize and meditate on the following verses from this chapter:

■ "Since we live by the Spirit, let us keep in step with the Spirit" (Galatians 5:25, NIV).

■ "We, who with unveiled faces all reflect the Lord's glory, are being transformed into His likeness with ever-increasing glory, which comes from the Lord, who is the Spirit" (2 Corinthians 3:18, NIV).

 Focus on the Presence of the Spirit. Prayerfully consider the following questions:

■ How can you know when you are moving toward His goal for you? Explain.

■ What word comes to mind when you consider your future? Why?

■ What was the single most important idea you gleaned from this book? Why?

 Walk in the Power of the Spirit. Ponder each of the following marks of walking in the Spirit. Prayerfully ask the Holy Spirit to develop these character traits in your life:

■ *Keeping in Step.* Be filled with the Spirit every single day.

■ *Overpowering in Praise.* Move toward challenges with a spirit of worship.

■ *Overcoming in Faith.* Trust God for victory when the world calls it impossible.

■ *Overflowing in Witness.* Share Christ from the abundance of your joy.

■ *Owning the Crown of Victory.* Run the race with your eyes on the final prize.

Ask the Spirit of God to fill you today, to fill you tomorrow, and to keep filling you as you eagerly embrace a lifetime of bearing fruit for Christ.

If the following prayer expresses the desire of your heart, make it your own and review it often.

My great Creator God and Savior, I bow before Your majesty with praise and thanksgiving to worship You. I am in awe of Your greatness, Your glory, Your mighty power, and Your unconditional love. For the rest of my life, with the enabling of the Holy Spirit, I surrender my all to love You, to trust You, to obey You, for You alone are worthy of my total, irrevocable allegiance. I invite You to live Your life in and through me, and pray that You will use me to bring honor and glory to Your matchless, incomparable name. I seek to win, build, train, and send others to keep fulfilling the Great Commandment to love and the Great Commission to take the gospel to all the world. I worship, praise, and adore You in the peerless name of Jesus. Amen.

Appendix A

Spiritual Gifts

Following are general definitions of the gifts of the Holy Spirit that are mentioned in 1 Corinthians 12 and 14, Romans 12, and Ephesians 4.

Wisdom (1 Corinthians 12:8)

Wisdom is a natural ability that is generally developed over a long period by all people. The spiritual gift of wisdom, however, while usually acquired as the believer matures spiritually, can also be instantaneous in nature. A Christian who has this gift can clearly discern the mind of Christ in applying specific knowledge to specific needs that arise within the body of Christ.

Knowledge (1 Corinthians 12:8)

Knowledge is another spiritual gift that has a counterpart in natural talent. Everyone is born with the natural ability to discover certain information and to formulate ideas from that information. But the Christian who has the spiritual gift of knowledge has a supernatural ability to discover, accumulate, analyze, and clarify information and ideas that are pertinent to the growth and well-being of the body of Christ.

Faith (1 Corinthians 12:9)

All believers are given faith in some measure and for certain reasons. For example, every believer is given the ability to have faith in Christ for his salvation. Each Christian is also to live by faith. Beyond that, faith is something that the believer may develop and apply in virtually every area of life.

This gift is the special ability to discern with extraordinary confidence the will and purposes of God as they relate to the growth and well-being of the body of Christ. It is evident in the lives of those ministers and laymen who do believe, as contrasted with the lives of those who do not.

Healing (1 Corinthians 12:9,28)

The gift of healing does not suggest that the recipient of the gift is given supernatural powers over the human body and over disease. Rather, it means that the individual is given the privilege of being the vessel through which God's works of healing are directed.

Healing in a strict sense is a miracle of God. This gift is available in its application to all Christians through the ministry of the elders of the church. This is described in James 5:14,15.

Doctors and others in the medical profession may acquire certain skills and develop certain natural abilities in the areas of medicine, but the healing itself is a miraculous wonder of the life process which is uniquely controlled by God. Many Christian doctors have natural and acquired abilities that are complemented by the gift of healing.

Miracles (1 Corinthians 12:10,28)

The gift of miracles is the supernatural ability given to certain believers through whom the Holy Spirit performs acts outside the ordinary laws of nature.

The Bible contains many illustrations of miracles, often performed by the Lord Himself. And in Revelation 11 we read that at a future time some believers will be given miraculous powers through the indwelling of the Holy Spirit. Nowhere in Scripture do we read that the granting of this very special gift has been temporarily held back by the Holy Spirit.

Prophecy (1 Corinthians 12:10,28; Romans 12:6; Ephesians 4:11)

The gift of prophecy is one of the most misunderstood of all the gifts.

Many people consider it the ability to foretell the future. The word literally means to "preach" or to proclaim the Word of God to others. A prophet, biblically, called a nation to repent and return to God. Like Dr. William Evans, most believers who have this gift find that it takes much time, hard work, and reliance on the power and control of the Holy Spirit to develop this gift.

Since so much of Scripture contains God's revelation of His future plans, the preaching of the Word from time to time includes dealing with things to come. Since the canon of Scripture is now "closed," or complete, such preaching on future things, if it is the result of being truly gifted, only confirms what the Bible says and does not add to the Scriptures.

Discerning of Spirits (1 Corinthians 12:10)
The gift of discerning of spirits is the supernatural ability of certain believers to discern whether things said and done by others are true or false, are of God or of Satan, are of the Holy Spirit or of the flesh. The writer of the Book of Hebrews tells us, "You will never be able to eat solid spiritual food and understand the deeper things of God's Word until you become better Christians and learn right from wrong by practicing doing right" (Hebrews 5:14, TLB).

This passage indicates to us that discernment of spirits is an ability which is learned over a period of time.

Tongues (1 Corinthians 12:10,28)
The gift of tongues is the supernatural ability to speak in a language or utterance never learned by the speaker. Like all the other gifts of the Holy Spirit, the gift of tongues has been given to the Church in order to glorify Christ and to build up the body of Christ (1 Corinthians 14:26). Unhappily, however, speaking in tongues has often become a divisive issue among many Christians.

Many others have written extensively (and exhaustively) on the issue of tongues, and it is doubtful that much could be written here that has not already been stated. Let me stress only two biblical principles: First, the gift of tongues must always be exercised in accordance with the biblical guidelines given in 1 Corinthians 14. Second, those who have this gift must exercise it in love and humility, and those who do not have this gift must accept with love those who claim to have it.

We must aim for equality and not sameness among the members of the body of Christ (2 Corinthians 8:14). And in so doing, we must seek first to glorify Christ and then to build up one another toward unity in the Holy Spirit. I suggest that you read again and again the passage of Scripture found in 1 Peter 4:7–19.

Interpretation of Tongues (1 Corinthians 12:10)
The gift of tongues may or may not be accompanied by the giving of another closely related gift, the interpretation of tongues. Whenever the gift of tongues is exercised in the presence of others, someone else must interpret (1 Corinthians 14:27,28), or the person speaking in tongues is to "pray also for the gift of knowing what he has said, so that he can tell people afterwards, plainly" (1 Corinthians 14:13, TLB).

Apostleship (1 Corinthians 12:28, Ephesians 4:11)
Some Christians are given special abilities to perform the functions of the office of the Church that is termed *apostle*, thus, the gift of apostleship. It was granted to the original twelve apostles, then others after them, including Paul (Acts 1:26; 14:14; Romans 1:1; 16:7; 1 Thessalonians 2:6).

Though we do not have people who could claim to be apostles in the original sense—those who had been eyewitnesses of the resurrected Christ (Acts 1:21–26)—today we would have those who may function much like an apostle. In a general sense, then, an apostle is one who is gifted by the Holy Spirit with the special ability to give leadership to a number of churches and to show supernatural wisdom and authority in spiritual matters that relate to those churches.

Teaching (1 Corinthians 12:28; Romans 12:7; Ephesians 4:11)
The gift of teaching is the supernatural ability to explain biblical truth to members of the body of Christ in such a way that they will be edified and able to apply it in their lives. This gift develops with maturity.

Teaching is a very common natural talent. But not all natural teaching is beneficial. Only the spiritual gift of teaching can bring about righteous results in the lives of others. This is true for two reasons.

First, the Christian's ability to teach is supernaturally imparted by the Holy Spirit. Since God is holy, any gift of His would be holy and could not be used in an unholy fashion, if properly exercised in the power and control of the Holy Spirit.

Second, for the Christian, the gift of teaching is the supernatural ability to teach *truths*. Since all truth is ultimately from God, it can have only a beneficial impact on the life of the student when properly applied.

Helps, Service, and Mercy (1 Corinthians 12:28; Romans 12:7,8)

The spiritual gifts of helps, service, and mercy are similar in many respects. All three are given for the building up of the body of Christ, but they differ slightly.

The gift of helps is characteristically more task-oriented. The gift of service is more people-oriented. The gift of mercy is extended usually to the infirm, the elderly, or the injured, who are unable to totally care for themselves.

Administration (1 Corinthians 12:28)

The gift of administration (called "governments" in some translations of the Bible) is the special ability given by the Holy Spirit to some believers enabling them to understand the objectives of a particular group within the body of Christ and to make and carry out plans for realizing those objectives.

We sometimes confuse this spiritual gift with the gift of leadership. While some leaders might also have the gift of administration, not all do. Conversely, not all who have the gift of administration have the gift of leadership.

Leadership (Romans 12:8)

The spiritual gift of leadership is the special ability given by the Holy Spirit to certain members of the body of Christ for the purpose of setting goals and motivating and directing the activities of others in working together toward accomplishing those goals.

An individual who has the gift of leadership but not of administration would do well to have supportive staff who are gifted in administration. Otherwise, and we see this too often, a leader will emerge who will establish goals and motivate people to work together to reach those goals only to fail because of poor planning, organization, direction, and controls.

Likewise, a well-organized local church that lacks a leader may flounder from misdirection or stagnancy, and its people may become frustrated and unfulfilled because of the slow rate or lack of progress in the life and growth of the church.

Exhortation (Romans 12:8)
The gift of exhortation is the special ability given by the Holy Spirit to certain members of the body of Christ to provide to groups or individuals words of comfort, consolation, encouragement, and counsel. The result of such counseling is to "build up" one another in Christ so that those exhorted will feel helped and healed.

Another term for exhortation is encouragement, which Hebrews 3:13 tells us to do: "Encourage one another daily" (NIV). Each of us is told to exercise this special ability, and therefore each of us, as Christians, is assured that the Holy Spirit will empower us with this gift: "For I can do everything God asks me to with the help of Christ who gives me the strength and power" (Philippians 4:13, TLB).

Giving (Romans 12:8)
In my many years with the ministry of Campus Crusade for Christ, I have seen the gift of giving demonstrated repeatedly. This gift is the supernatural ability to acquire money to give to others for the sole purpose of carrying out the work of God.

Those who possess this gift are among the happiest and most cheerful people I know. This is proof of the Lord's promise that "it is more blessed to give than to receive" (Acts 20:35).

Evangelism (Ephesians 4:11)

Ephesians 4:11 refers to evangelism as an office; however, I believe it is also a special ability given by the Holy Spirit to certain believers, though granted in different and varying amounts. While some are given this special ability, the Bible teaches that the Church is commissioned to preach the gospel throughout the entire world (Matthew 28:19,20), and that the Lord promised that the Holy Spirit would indwell all believers for the specific purpose of witnessing for Him (Acts 1:8).

Out of love for the Lord and in obedience to His command, all believers are to be witnesses for Him as a way of life. The supernaturalness of this gift lies in our motivation, which is prompted by the Holy Spirit, to want to share Christ, and in the power of the Holy Spirit to open minds to the gospel when it is shared. All Christians should share Christ with others. Those who are more gifted in evangelism should devote even more time reaching others for Christ.

Pastoring (Ephesians 4:11)

The office of pastor, as listed in Ephesians 4, indicates that certain members of the body of Christ are given special abilities by the Holy Spirit to pastor or "shepherd" the members of that unit of the Church. This gift gives one the ability to care for the interests of those believers whom God has committed to his care.

The gift of pastoring, however, is not limited to those who hold the church office of pastor. A lay person who has a strong desire to disciple or shepherd a group of people in his home may well have the gift of pastoring. All too often the entire responsibility of pastoring in a local church is limited to the office of pastor. Among the most dynamic local churches I have seen are those in which the gift of pastoring is recognized among the laity and its practice is encouraged.

Total Availability to God

As we have seen in this appendix, many of the spiritual gifts are similar in nature, and many times individuals may have two or more gifts that greatly complement one another. Again, I want to say that knowing what our spiritual gifts are is much less important than being available to God at all times and in every way to build up the body of Christ.

Remember too that spiritual gifts are not a mark of spirituality. That was obvious in the Corinthian church, one of the most carnal churches of all, and yet one in which there was a wrongly motivated overemphasis on spiritual gifts.

Finally, we can know that we are living Spirit-filled lives, not by the manifestation of spiritual gifts but when the *fruit* of the Spirit, the greatest of which is love, becomes increasingly evident in our lives.

Would You Like to Know God Personally?

The following four principles will help you discover how to know God personally and experience the abundant life He promised.

1 *God **loves** you and created you to know Him personally.*

God's Love

"God so loved the world that He gave His one and only Son, that who-ever believes in Him shall not perish but have eternal life" (John 3:16, NIV).

God's Plan

"Now this is eternal life: that they may know you, the only true God, and Jesus Christ, whom you have sent" (John 17:3, NIV).

What prevents us from knowing God personally?

2 *Man is **sinful** and **separated** from God, so we cannot know Him personally or experience His love.*

Man Is Sinful

"All have sinned and fall short of the glory of God" (Romans 3:23).

Man was created to have fellowship with God; but, because of his own stubborn self-will, he chose to go his own independent way and fellowship with God was broken. This self-will, characterized by an attitude of active rebellion or passive indifference, is an evidence of what the Bible calls sin.

Man Is Separated

"The wages of sin is death" [spiritual separation from God] (Romans 6:23).

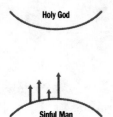

This diagram illustrates that God is holy and man is sinful. A great gulf separates the two. The arrows illustrate that man is continually trying to reach God and the abundant life through his own efforts, such as a good life, philosophy, or religion—but he inevitably fails.

The third principle explains the only way to bridge this gulf...

3 *Jesus Christ is God's only provision for man's sin. Through Him alone we can know God personally and experience God's love.*

He Died In Our Place

"God demonstrates His own love toward us, in that while we were yet sinners, Christ died for us" (Romans 5:8).

He Rose from the Dead

"Christ died for our sins...He was buried...He was raised on the third day according to the Scriptures...He appeared to Peter, then to the twelve. After that He appeared to more than five hundred..." (1 Corinthians 15:3–6).

He Is the Only Way to God

"Jesus said to him, 'I am the way, and the truth, and the life; no one comes to the Father, but through Me'" (John 14:6).

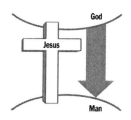

This diagram illustrates that God has bridged the gulf that separates us from Him by sending His Son, Jesus Christ, to die on the cross in our place to pay the penalty for our sins.

It is not enough just to know these three truths...

4 *We must individually receive Jesus Christ as Savior and Lord; then we can know God personally and experience His love.*

We Must Receive Christ
"As many as received Him, to them He gave the right to become children of God, even to those who believe in His name" (John 1:12).

We Receive Christ Through Faith
"By grace you have been saved through faith; and that not of yourselves, it is the gift of God; not as a result of works, that no one should boast" (Ephesians 2:8,9).

When We Receive Christ, We Experience a New Birth
(Read John 3:1–8.)

We Receive Christ Through Personal Invitation
[Christ speaking] "Behold, I stand at the door and knock; if anyone hears My voice and opens the door, I will come in to him" (Revelation 3:20).

Receiving Christ involves turning to God from self (repentance) and trusting Christ to come into our lives to forgive our sins and to make us what He wants us to be. Just to agree intellectually that Jesus Christ is the Son of God and that He died on the cross for our sins is not enough. Nor is it enough to have an emotional experience. We receive Jesus Christ by faith, as an act of the will.

These two circles represent two kinds of lives:

Self-Directed Life
S – Self is on the throne
† – Christ is outside the life
● – Interests are directed by self, often
    resulting in discord and frustration

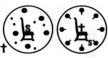

Christ-Directed Life
† – Christ is in the life and on the throne
S – Self is yielding to Christ
● – Interests are directed by Christ,
    resulting in harmony with God's plan

Which circle best represents your life?

Which circle would you like to have represent your life?

The following explains how you can receive Christ:

You Can Receive Christ Right Now by Faith Through Prayer
(Prayer is talking with God)

God knows your heart and is not so concerned with your words as He is with the attitude of your heart. The following is a suggested prayer:

> *Lord Jesus, I want to know You personally. Thank You for dying on the cross for my sins. I open the door of my life and receive You as my Savior and Lord. Thank You for forgiving my sins and giving me eternal life. Take control of the throne of my life. Make me the kind of person You want me to be.*

Does this prayer express the desire of your heart? If it does, I invite you to pray this prayer right now, and Christ will come into your life, as He promised.

How to Know That Christ Is in Your Life

Did you receive Christ into your life? According to His promise in Revelation 3:20, where is Christ right now in relation to you? Christ said that He would come into your life and be your friend so you can know Him personally. Would He mislead you? On what authority do you know that God has answered your prayer? (The trustworthiness of God Himself and His Word.)

The Bible Promises Eternal Life to All Who Receive Christ

"God has given us eternal life, and this life is in His Son. He who has the Son has the life; he who does not have the Son of God does not have the life" (1 John 5:11,12).

Thank God often that Christ is in your life and that He will never leave you (Hebrews 13:5). You can know on the basis of His promise that Christ lives in you and that you have eternal life from the very moment you invite Him in. He will not deceive you.

An important reminder...

Do Not Depend on Feelings

The promise of God's Word, the Bible—not our feelings—is our authority. The Christian lives by faith (trust) in the trustworthiness of God Himself and His Word. This train diagram illustrates the relationship among fact (God and His Word), faith (our trust in God and His Word), and feeling (the result of our faith and obedience). (Read John 14:21.)

The train will run with or without the caboose. However, it would be useless to attempt to pull the train by the caboose. In the same way, as Christians we do not depend on feelings or emotions, but we place our faith (trust) in the trustworthiness of God and the promises of His Word.

Now That You Have Entered Into a
Personal Relationship with Christ

The moment you received Christ by faith, as an act of the will, many things happened, including the following:

- Christ came into your life (Revelation 3:20; Colossians 1:27).
- Your sins were forgiven (Colossians 1:14).
- You became a child of God (John 1:12).
- You received eternal life (John 5:24).
- You began the great adventure for which God created you (John 10:10).

Can you think of anything more wonderful that could happen to you than entering into a personal relationship with Jesus Christ? Would you like to thank God in prayer right now for what He has done for you? By thanking God, you demonstrate your faith.

To enjoy your new relationship with God...

Suggestions for Christian Growth

Spiritual growth results from trusting Jesus Christ. A life of faith will enable you to trust God increasingly with every detail of your life, and to practice the following:

G *Go* to God in prayer daily (John 15:7).

R *Read* God's Word daily (Acts 17:11); begin with the Gospel of John.

O *Obey* God moment by moment (John 14:21).

W *Witness* for Christ by your life and words (Matthew 4:19; John 15:8).

T *Trust* God for every detail of your life (1 Peter 5:7).

H *Holy Spirit*—allow Him to control and empower your daily life and witness (Galatians 5:16,17; Acts 1:8; Ephesians 5:18).

Fellowship in a Good Church

God's Word instructs us not to forsake "the assembling of ourselves together" (Hebrews 10:25). If you do not belong to a church, do not wait to be invited. Take the initiative; call the pastor of a nearby church where Christ is honored and His Word is preached. Start this week, and make plans to attend regularly.

Appendix C

Satisfied?

Satisfaction: (n.) fulfillment of one's needs, longings, or desires

What words would you use to describe your current experience as a Christian?

Growing	Frustrated
Disappointing	Fulfilled
Forgiven	Stuck
Struggling	Joyful
Defeated	Exciting
Up and down	Empty
Discouraged	Duty
Intimate	Mediocre
Painful	Dynamic
Guilty	Vital
So-so	Others?

Do you desire more? Jesus said, "If anyone is thirsty, let him come to me and drink. Whoever believes in me, as the Scripture has said, streams of living water will flow from within him" (John 7:37,38).

What did Jesus mean? John, the biblical author, went on to explain, "By this he meant the Spirit, whom those who believed in him were later to receive. Up to that time the Spirit had not been given, since Jesus had not yet been glorified" (John 7:39).

231

Jesus promised that God's Holy Spirit would satisfy the thirst, or deepest longings, of all who believe in Jesus Christ. However, many Christians do not understand the Holy Spirit or how to experience Him in their daily lives.

The following principles will help you understand and enjoy God's Spirit.

The Divine Gift

Divine: (adj.) given by God

God has given us His Spirit so that we can experience intimacy with Him and enjoy all He has for us.

The Holy Spirit is the source of our deepest satisfaction.

The Holy Spirit is God's permanent presence with us.

Jesus said, "I will ask the Father, and he will give you another Counselor to be with you forever—the Spirit of truth" (John 14:16,17).

The Holy Spirit enables us to understand and experience all God has given us.

"We have not received the spirit of the world but the Spirit who is from God, that we may understand what God has freely given us" (1 Corinthians 2:12).

The Holy Spirit enables us to experience many things:

- A genuine new spiritual life (John 3:1–8).
- The assurance of being a child of God (Romans 8:15,16).
- The infinite love of God (Romans 5:5; Ephesians 3:18,19).

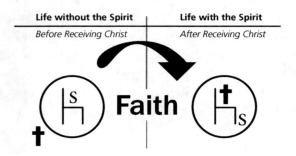

Life without the Spirit	Life with the Spirit
Before Receiving Christ	*After Receiving Christ*

Faith

"The man without the Spirit does not accept the things that come from the Spirit of God, for they are foolishness to him, and he cannot understand them, because they are spiritually discerned" (1 Corinthians 2:14).

"The spiritual man makes judgments about all things…We have the mind of Christ" (1 Corinthians 2:15,16).

"But those who are controlled by the Holy Spirit think about things that please the Spirit" (Romans 8:5, NLT).

Why are many Christians not satisfied in their experience with God?

The Present Danger
Danger: (n.) a thing that may cause injury, loss, or pain
We cannot experience intimacy with God and enjoy all He has for us if we fail to depend on His Spirit.

People who trust in their own efforts and strength to live the Christian life will experience failure and frustration, as will those who live to please themselves rather than God.

We cannot live the Christian life in our own strength.
"Are you so foolish? After beginning with the Spirit, are you now trying to attain your goal by human effort?" (Galatians 3:3).

We cannot enjoy all God desires for us if we live by our self-centered desires.
"For the sinful nature desires what is contrary to the Spirit, and the Spirit what is contrary to the sinful nature. They are in conflict with each other, so that you do not do what you want" (Galatians 5:17).

Three Kinds of Lifestyles

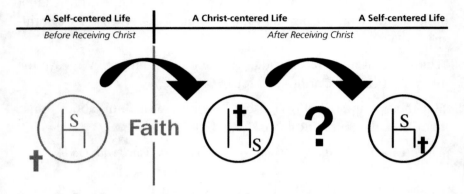

"Brothers, I could not address you as spiritual, but as worldly—mere infants in Christ. I gave you milk, not solid food, for you were not yet ready for it. Indeed, you are still not ready. You are still worldly. For since there is jealousy and quarreling among you, are you not worldly? Are you not acting like mere men?" (1 Corinthians 3:1–3).

How can we develop a lifestyle of depending on the Spirit?

The Intimate Journey

Journey: (n.) any course from one experience to another

By walking in the Spirit we increasingly experience intimacy with God and enjoy all He has for us.

Walking in the Spirit moment by moment is a lifestyle. It is learning to depend upon the Holy Spirit for His abundant resources as a way of life.

As we walk in the Spirit, we have the ability to live a life pleasing to God.

"So I say, live by the Spirit, and you will not gratify the desires of the sinful nature...Since we live by the Spirit, let us keep in step with the Spirit" (Galatians 5:16,25).

As we walk in the Spirit, we experience intimacy with God and all He has for us.

"But the fruit of the Spirit is love, joy, peace, patience, kindness, goodness, faithfulness, gentleness and self-control" (Galatians 5:22,23).

The Christ-centered Life

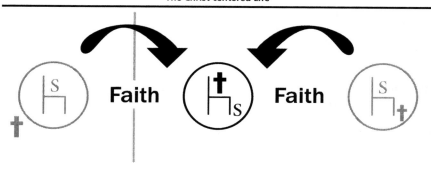

Faith (trust in God and His promises) is the only way a Christian can live by the Spirit.

Spiritual breathing is a powerful word picture which can help you experience moment-by-moment dependence upon the Spirit.

Exhale: Confess your sin the moment you become aware of it—agree with God concerning it and thank Him for His forgiveness, according to 1 John 1:9 and Hebrews 10:1–25. Confession requires repentance —a change in attitude and action.

Inhale: Surrender control of your life to Christ, and rely upon the Holy Spirit to fill you with His presence and power by faith, according to His command (Ephesians 5:18) and promise (1 John 5:14,15).

How does the Holy Spirit fill us with His power?

The Empowering Presence
Empower: (v.) to give ability to
We are filled with the Spirit by faith, enabling us to experience intimacy with God and enjoy all He has for us.

The essence of the Christian life is what God does in and through us, not what we do for God. Christ's life is reproduced in the believer by the power of the Holy Spirit. To be filled with the Spirit is to be directed and empowered by Him.

By faith, we experience God's power through the Holy Spirit.
"I pray that out of his glorious riches he may strengthen you with power through his Spirit in your inner being, so that Christ may dwell in your hearts through faith" (Ephesians 3:16,17).

Three important questions to ask yourself:

1. Am I ready now to surrender control of my life to our Lord Jesus Christ? (Romans 12:1,2).

2. Am I ready now to confess my sins? (1 John 1:9). Sin grieves God's Spirit (Ephesians 4:30). But God in His love has forgiven all of your sins—past, present, and future—because Christ has died for you.

3. Do I sincerely desire to be directed and empowered by the Holy Spirit? (John 7:37–39).

By faith claim the fullness of the Spirit according to His command and promise:

God COMMANDS us to be filled with the Spirit.
"...be filled with the Spirit" (Ephesians 5:18).

God PROMISES He will always answer when we pray according to His will.
"This is the confidence we have in approaching God: that if we ask anything according to his will, he hears us. And if we know that he

hears us—whatever we ask—we know that we have what we asked of him" (1 John 5:14,15).

How to pray to be filled with the Holy Spirit . . .

The Turning Point

Turning point: time when a decisive change occurs

We are filled with the Holy Spirit by faith alone.

Sincere prayer is one way of expressing our faith. The following is a suggested prayer:

> Dear Father, I need You. I acknowledge that I have sinned against You by directing my own life. I thank You that You have forgiven my sins through Christ's death on the cross for me. I now invite Christ to again take His place on the throne of my life. Fill me with the Holy Spirit as You commanded me to be filled, and as You promised in Your Word that You would do if I asked in faith. I pray this in the name of Jesus. I now thank You for filling me with the Holy Spirit and directing my life.

Does this prayer express the desire of your heart? If so, you can pray right now and trust God to fill you with His Holy Spirit.

How to know that you are filled by the Holy Spirit

- Did you ask God to fill you with the Holy Spirit?

- Do you know that you are now filled with the Holy Spirit?

- On what authority? (On the trustworthiness of God Himself and His Word: Hebrews 11:6; Romans 14:22,23.)

As you continue to depend on God's Spirit moment by moment you will experience and enjoy intimacy with God and all He has for you— a truly rich and satisfying life.

An important reminder . . .

Do Not Depend on Feelings

The promise of God's Word, the Bible—not our feelings—is our authority. The Christian lives by faith (trust) in the trustworthiness of

God Himself and His Word. Flying in an airplane can illustrate the relationship among fact (God and His Word), faith (our trust in God and His Word), and feeling (the result of our faith and obedience) (John 14:21).

To be transported by an airplane, we must place our faith in the trustworthiness of the aircraft and the pilot who flies it. Our feelings of confidence or fear do not affect the ability of the airplane to transport us, though they do affect how much we enjoy the trip. In the same way, we as Christians do not depend on feelings or emotions, but we place our faith (trust) in the trustworthiness of God and the promises of His Word.

Now That You are Filled with the Holy Spirit

Thank God that the Spirit will enable you:

- To glorify Christ with your life (John 16:14).

- To grow in your understanding of God and His Word (1 Corinthians 2:14,15).

- To live a life pleasing to God (Galatians 5:16–23).

Remember the promise of Jesus:

"But you will receive power when the Holy Spirit comes on you; and you will be my witnesses in Jerusalem, and in all Judea and Samaria, and to the ends of the earth" (Acts 1:8).

If you would like additional resources on the Holy Spirit, please go to www.nlpdirect.com.

Adapted from *Have You Made the Wonderful Discovery of the Spirit-filled Life?* written by Bill Bright, © 1966. Published by NewLife Publications, P.O. Box 593684, Orlando, FL 32859.

Appendix D

How to Know God's Will

One of the most frequent questions people ask me is how to determine God's will for their life. This letter, written to a fictitious Paul Brown, contains the basic counsel that I give to students and adults about how to know God's will for their life according to the "sound mind" principle of Scripture.

Mr. Paul V. Brown
The Graduate House
University of California
Los Angeles, California 90024

Dear Paul:

Thank you for your recent letter sharing some of the exciting experiences which you are having in your new and adventuresome life with Christ.

When I read that part of your letter in which you expressed the desire to invest your life fully for Christ, I paused to give thanks to the Lord, first, for His great love and faithful direction in the lives of all who will trust Him, and second, for your response to His love and your willingness to trust Him with every detail of your life.

It is at this crucial point that many Christians deprive themselves of the full, abundant, and purposeful life that the Lord Jesus promised in John 10:10. Failing to comprehend the true character and nature of God—His absolute love, grace, wisdom, power and holiness—many Christians have foolishly chosen to live according to their own plans rather than consider and do the will of God. Some have such a distorted view of God that they think of Him as a tyrant whom one must either appease by their actions or experience His wrath, as those who worship a pagan god. Since they are afraid of Him, they cannot love and trust Him. This is sometimes true of individuals who have transferred to God their fear of an earthly father who may have been overly strict, unduly demanding, or even tyrannical.

In all fairness I should say that there are many sincere Christians who want to do the will of God but who do not know how to go about discovering His will for their lives.

A young college graduate came to me recently for counsel concerning God's will for his life. "How can I know what God wants me to do?" he asked. Briefly, I explained the safest approach to knowing the will of God—to follow what I have chosen to call the "sound mind" principle of Scripture. In less than an hour, by following the suggestions contained in this letter, this young man discovered what he had been seeking for years. He knew not only the work that God wanted him to do, but the very organization with which he was to be affiliated.

Now you may ask, "What is the 'sound mind' principle of Scripture?' In 2 Timothy 1:7 we are told that "God has not given us the spirit of fear, but of power, and of love and of a sound mind." The sound mind referred to in this verse means a well-balanced mind, a mind that is under the control of the Holy Spirit, "remade" according to Romans 12:1,2: "Therefore, my brothers, I implore you by God's mercies to offer your very selves to Him, a living sacrifice, dedicated and fit for His acceptance, the worship offered by mind and heart. Adapt yourselves no longer to the pattern of the present world, but let your minds be remade and your whole nature thus transformed. Then you will be able to discern the will of God and to know it is good, acceptable and perfect" (NEB).

There is a vast difference between the inclination of the natural or carnal man to use "common sense" and that of the spiritual man to follow the sound mind principle. One, for understanding, depends upon the wisdom of man without benefit of God's wisdom and pow - er; the other, having the mind of Christ, receives wisdom and guidance from God moment by moment through faith.

Are your decisions as a Christian based upon unpredictable emotions and chance circumstances, the common sense of the natural man? Or do you make your decisions according to the sound mind principle of Scripture?

Through the years, as I have counseled with many Christians, the question most frequently asked has been, "How can I know the will of God for my life?" Inevitably, the majority of Christians who come for counsel are looking for some dramatic or cataclysmic revelation from God by which they will know His plan. Without minimizing the importance of feelings, which Jesus promised in John 14:21 will follow as a result of obedience, more emphasis needs to be placed upon the importance of the sound mind that God has given us. Multitudes of sincere Christians are wasting their lives, immobile and impotent, as they wait for some unusual or dramatic word from God.

The Scripture assures us that God has given us a "sound mind." Thus, a Christian who has yielded his life fully to Christ can be assured of sanctified reasoning and a balanced, disciplined mind. Also, God has promised to give His children wisdom according to James 1:5–7. Further, we can know with settled and absolute assurance that when we pray according to the will of God, He will always hear and grant our petitions (1 John 5:14,15). Since the Christian is to live by faith, and faith comes through an understanding of the Word of God, it is impossible to overemphasize the importance of Scripture in the lives of those who would know and do the will of God.

If you would like to know the will of God for your life according to the sound mind principle of Scripture, may I suggest that you follow this bit of logic. Consider these questions: First, "Why did Jesus come?" He came "to seek and save the lost" (Luke 19:10). Then, "What is the greatest experience of your life?" If you are a Christian, your answer quite obviously will be, "Coming to know Christ personally as my Savior and Lord." Finally, "What is the greatest thing that you can do to help others?" The answer is again obvious, "Introducing them to Christ."

Jesus came to seek and to save the lost, and every Christian is under divine orders to be a faithful witness for Christ. Jesus said, "By this My Father is glorified, that you bear much fruit; so you will be

241

My disciples" (John 15:8, NKJ). It logically follows that the most im -
portant thing I can possibly do as a Christian is to allow the Lord Jesus
Christ in all of His resurrection power to have complete, unhindered
control of my life. Otherwise He cannot continue seeking and saving
the lost through me.

Thus, every sincere Christian will want to make his God-given time,
talents, and treasure available to Christ so that his fullest potential will
be realized for Him. For one Christian, the talent God has given him
may be preaching, evangelism, or teaching; for another, it may be
business; for another, the ministry or missions; for another, home-
making, as expressed in Romans 12; 1 Corinthians 12; 1 Corinthians
14; Ephesians 4; and other Scriptures.

As you evaluate the talents that God has given you in relation to
your training, personality, and other qualities, may I suggest that you
take a sheet of paper and make a list of the most logical ways through
which your life can be used to accomplish the most for the glory of
God. With the desire to put His will above all else, list the pros and
cons of each opportunity. Where and how, according to the sound
mind principle, can the Lord Jesus Christ through your yielded life
accomplish the most in continuing His great ministry of seeking and
saving the lost? Like my young friend, you will find that such a proce-
dure will inevitably result in positive actions leading to God's perfect
will for your life. But note a word of caution. The sound mind principle is not valid unless certain factors exist:

1. There must be no unconfessed sin in your life; following 1 John
   1:9 takes care of that: "If we confess our sins, [God] is faithful and
   just to forgive us our sins and to cleanse us from all unrighteous-
   ness."

2. Your life must be fully dedicated to Christ according to Romans
   12:1,2, and you must be filled with the Holy Spirit in obedience to
   the command of Ephesians 5:18. As in the case of our salvation,
   we are filled and controlled by the Spirit through faith.

3. In order to know the will of God, you must walk in the Spirit
   (abide in Christ) moment by moment. You place your faith in the
   trustworthiness of God with the confidence that the Lord is direct-

ing and will continue to direct your life according to His promise that the "steps of a righteous man are ordered of the Lord." For, "as you have therefore received Christ Jesus the Lord, so walk in Him." How? By faith, by placing your complete trust in Him. Now, you must go on walking by faith. Remember, "that which is not of faith is sin," "the just shall live by faith," and "without faith it is impossible to please God." Faith is the catalyst for all our Christian relationships.

The counsel of others should be prayerfully considered, especially that of mature dedicated Christians who know the Word of God and are able to relate the proper use of Scripture to your need. However, care should be taken not to make the counsel of others a crutch. Although God often speaks to us through other Christians, we are admonished to place our trust in Him. In Psalm 37 we are told to delight ourselves in the Lord and He will give us the desires of our hearts, to commit our ways unto the Lord, to trust Him and He will bring it to pass. Also, in Proverbs 3 we are told, "Trust in the Lord with all thine heart; and lean not unto thine own understanding. In alt thy ways acknowledge Him, and He shall direct thy paths."

God never contradicts Himself. He never leads us to do anything contrary to the commands of His Word; for according to Philippians 2:13, "It is God who is at work within you, giving you the will and the power to achieve His purpose" (Phillips).

Through the centuries sincere religious men have suggested spiritual formulas for discovering the will of God. Some are valid; others are unscriptural and misleading. For example, a young seminary graduate came to see me. He was investigating various possibilities of Christian service and had come to discuss the ministry of Campus Crusade for Christ. Applying the sound mind principle to his quest, I asked him, "In what way do you expect God to reveal His place of service for you?"

He replied, "I am following the 'closed door' policy. A few months ago I began to investigate several opportunities for Christian service. The Lord has now closed the door on all but two, one of which is Campus Crusade for Christ. If the door to accept a call to a particular church closes, I shall know that God wants me in Campus Crusade."

Many sincere Christians follow this illogical and unscriptural method, often with most unsatisfactory and frustrating consequences. Don't misunderstand; God may and often does close doors in the life of an active, Spirit-controlled Christian. This was true in the experience of the apostle Paul. As recorded in Acts 16:6–10, he was forbidden by the Spirit to go into Bithynia because God wanted him in Macedonia. My reference to "closed door" policies does not preclude such experiences, but refers to a careless hit-or-miss attitude without the careful evaluation of all the issues.

This approach is illogical because it allows elements of chance to influence a decision rather than a careful, intelligent evaluation of all the factors involved. It is unscriptural in that it fails to employ the God-given faculties of reason that are controlled by the Holy Spirit.

Further, the closed-door policy is in error because it seeks God's will through the process of elimination rather than seeking God's best first. It should be understood that true faith is established on the basis of fact. Therefore, vital faith in God is emphasized rather than minimized through employing Spirit-controlled reason. In making decisions, some sincere Christians rely almost entirely upon impressions or hunches, fearful that if they use their mental faculties they will not exercise adequate faith and thus will grieve the Holy Spirit.

There are those who assume that a door has been closed simply because of difficulties that have been encountered. Yet, experience has taught and Scripture confirms that God's richest blessings often follow periods of greatest testing. This might include financial needs, loss of health, objection of loved ones, and criticism of fellow Christians. God's blessing is promised, however, only to those who are obedient, who keep on trying, who demonstrate their faith in God's faithfulness. The apparent defeat of the cross was followed by the victory of the resurrection.

An acceptable consideration for discussing God's will contains four basic factors somewhat similar to the sound mind principle. God's will is revealed in (1) the authority of Scripture, (2) providential circumstances, (3) conviction based upon reason, and (4) impressions of the Holy Spirit upon our minds. However, such an appraisal is safer with a mature Christian than with a new or carnal Christian, and there is always the danger of misunderstanding impressions.

You must know the source of leading before responding to it. To the inexperienced, what appears to be the leading of God may not be from Him at all but from "the rulers of darkness of this world." Satan and his helpers often disguise themselves as "angels of light" by performing "miracles and signs," by "foretelling events," etc. The enemy of our souls is a master counterfeiter.

Remember, just as the turning of the steering wheel of an automobile does not alter its direction unless it is moving, so God cannot direct our lives unless we are moving for Him. I challenge you to begin employing the sound mind principle today in all your relationships. Apply it to the investment of your time, your talents, and your treasure, for this principle applies to everything you do in this life. Every Christian should take spiritual inventory regularly by asking himself these questions: Is my time being invested in such a way that the largest possible number of people are being introduced to Christ? Are my talents being invested to the full so that the largest possible number of people are being introduced to Christ? Is my money, my treasure, being invested in such a way as to introduce the greatest number of people to Christ?

Every Christian is admonished to be a good steward of his God-given time, talents, and treasure. Therefore, these investments must not be dictated by tradition, habit, or emotions. Every investment of time, talent, and treasure, unless otherwise directed by the Holy Spirit, should be determined by the sound mind principle of Scripture according to 2 Timothy 1:7.

Regarding the questions asked by your girlfriend, the same principle applies to her. How does this sound mind principle apply in the case of a secretary, a homemaker, an invalid, or one who, because of circumstances beyond her control, does not have direct contact with men and women who are in need of Christ?

First, each Christian must be a witness for Christ. This is simply an act of obedience for which one need not possess the gift of evangelism. If normal day-to-day contacts do not provide opportunities to witness for Christ, an obedient Christian will make opportunities through personal contacts, church calling, letter writing, etc. Two of the most radiant, effective, and fruitful Christians I have known were bedridden invalids who, though in constant pain, bore a powerful witness for Christ to all—stranger and friend alike. "That which is most in our hearts will be most on our lips" was demonstrated in their lives.

Second, a careful evaluation should be given to determine if God may not have a better position for her. Again, the sound mind principle applies. For example, a secretary in a secular organization may have less opportunity to make her life count for the Lord. It may be that God wants to use an individual's talents in a Christian organization. (I happen to know that there is a great scarcity of qualified secretarial help in many Christian organizations, including Campus Crusade for Christ.) One should be very careful, however, not to run from what appears to be a difficult assignment. A careful appraisal of one's present responsibilities, with this new understanding of God's leading, may well reveal a great potential for Christ.

Quite obviously, members of an office staff do not have as much contact with men and women who are in need of our Savior as those who are working on the campus or conducting evangelistic meetings. However, according to the sound mind principle, if these staff members' lives are fully dedicated to Christ, they can make a vital contribution to the effectiveness of any Christian ministry. By relieving others who have the gift of evangelism without the talent for business or secretarial responsibilities, the overall ministry for Christ in such an organization is strengthened greatly. In this way, they can more fully utilize their talents in helping to seek and save the lost.

For example, a dedicated member of the secretarial staff of the worldwide ministry of Campus Crusade for Christ is just as vital to the success of the campus strategy as those who are working on the campus. My own personal ministry has been greatly increased by the dedicated efforts of several secretaries who are more concerned about winning students to Christ than their own personal pleasure.

One further word of explanation must be given. It is true that God still reveals His will to some men and women in dramatic ways, but this should be considered the exception rather than the rule. God still leads men today as He has through the centuries. Philip, the deacon, was holding a successful campaign in Samaria. The sound mind principle would have directed him to continue his campaign. However, God overruled by a special revelation, and Philip was led by the Holy Spirit to preach Christ to the Ethiopian eunuch. According to tradition, God used the Ethiopian eunuch to communicate the message of our living Lord to his own country.

Living according to the sound mind principle allows for such dramatic leadings of God, but we are not to wait for such revelations before we start moving for Christ. Faith must have an object. A Christian's faith is built upon the authority of God's Word supported by historical fact and not upon any shallow emotional experience. However, a Christian's trust in God's will revealed in His Word will result in decisions that are made by following the sound mind principle. The confirmation may come in various ways according to many factors, including the personality of the individual involved. Usually, the confirmation is a quiet, peaceful assurance that you are doing what God wants you to do, with expectancy that God will use you to bear "much fruit."

As any sincere Christian gives himself to a diligent study of the Scripture and allows a loving, all-wise, sovereign God and Father to control his life, feelings will inevitably result. Thus, the end result of a life that is lived according to the sound mind principle is the most joyful, abundant, and fruitful life of all. Expect the Lord Jesus Christ to draw men to Himself through you. As you begin each day, ac - knowledge the fact that you belong to Him. Thank Him for the fact that He lives within you. Invite Him to use your mind to think His thoughts, your heart to express His love, your lips to speak His truth. Ask Jesus to be at home in your life and to walk around in your body in order that He may continue seeking and saving souls through you.

It is my sincere prayer, Paul, that you may know this kind of life, that you may fully appropriate all that God has given to you as your rightful heritage in Christ. I shall look forward to hearing more from you concerning your personal application of this sound mind principle.

Warmly in Christ,
Bill Bright

End Notes

Chapter 2

1. George Barna, Bel Air Presbyterian Church, Bel Air, California, 2000.
2. W. E. Vine, *Vine's Expository Dictionary of New Testament Words*, (McCLean, VA: MacDonald Publishing Company), p. 210.
3. "Holy Spirit," www.autoillustrator.com.

Chapter 3

1. "Holy Spirit, filling," Biblical Studies Foundation, www.bible.org/illus/h/h-43.htm.
2. Ibid.
3. R. Kent Hughes, *1001 Great Stories and "Quotes,"* (Wheaton, IL: Tyndale, 1998), p. 207.

Chapter 7

1. *The Hiding Place*, "Illustration for Biblical Preaching," #1349, (Suffering, www.autoillustrator.com).
2. Dietrich Bonhoeffer, submitted by Jim Haley, *Parables, Etc.*, March 1984 (Platteville, CO: Saratoga Press).
3. Jack Canfield, Mark Victor Hansen, eds., *A 2nd Helping of Chicken Soup for the Soul* (Dearfield Beach, FL: Heath Communications, Inc., 1995), pp. 309–310.
4. C. H. Spurgeon, "Illustration for Biblical Preaching," #1163 (Comfort, www.autoillustrator.com).

5. "Illustration for Biblical Preaching," #588 (Comfort, www.autoillus-trator.com).

6. Joni Eareckson, *Joni* (Boston: G. K. Hall, 1979).

Chapter 8
1. Witness by Life, "Illustration for Biblical Preaching," *Patience*, www.autoillustrator.com.

Chapter 10
1. J. I. Packer, *Keep in Step with the Spirit* (Grand Rapids, MI: Fleming H. Revell, 1984), p. 83.

Chapter 12
1. Lee Strobel, *The Case for Faith* (Grand Rapids, MI: Zondervan Publishing House, 2000), p. 162.

Chapter 13
1. Charles Stanley, *The Wonderful Spirit-Filled Life* (Nashville, TN: Thomas Nelson Publishers, 1992), p. 101.

2. "Illustration for Biblical Preaching, #1295, "joy," www.autoillustrator.com.

3. Booker T. Washington, "Up From Slavery," *Parables Etc.*, September 1986 (Platteville, CO: Saratoga Press).

Chapter 14
1. Tom Carter, comp., *2200 Quotations from the writings of Charles H. Spurgeon.* (Grand Rapids, MI: Baker Books, 1988), pp. 101–2.

Resources

First Love: Renewing Your Passion for God

"I have admired Bill Bright as a champion for world evangelism and Spirit-filled living," says Dr. David Jeremiah. "Not until I read his new book, *First Love*, did I understand completely the spiritual dynamic that has driven him for the fifty years of his ministry." Find out how you too can return to a "first love" relationship with the Lord in Bill Bright's book. ISBN 1-56399-188-8

Heaven or Hell: The Ultimate Choice

"Where will I go when I die?" The most important question in life only has two possible answers: heaven or hell. And the choice is ours to make. Get the facts. Eternity is a long time to regret a wrong decision. Good decisions are made with good facts. You can know the facts about heaven or hell—what God Himself says in the Bible—in this new book from Bill Bright. ISBN 1-56399-191-8

Written by the Hand of God

Although all of Scripture is inspired by God, only the Ten Command-ments were truly written by the hand of God. They were given to us on Mount Sinai as pure principles of godly living. In this practical book, Bill Bright shows how the Old Testament truths about God's standard of holiness are reaffirmed in the New Testament and how the Ten Commandments are relevant to us today. ISBN 1-56399-165-9

A Child of the King

This first novel in a three-book series is a timeless tale of a kingdom turned away from the sun, a brave but vulnerable orphan, a diabolical foe and a king whose love never ends. The story could be your own. Written in the beloved, allegorical tradition of C. S. Lewis and J. R. R. Tolkien, *A Child of the King* takes you on a quest for truth, virtue and self-worth in a dark and hostile world. 1-56399-150-0

Satisfied?

In this new version of Campus Crusade for Christ's popular tract *Have You Made the Wonderful Discovery of the Spirit-filled Life?*, you will find a wonderful tool for helping other Christians understand what it means to walk in the power of the Holy Spirit—and enjoy a free, abundant life. ISBN 1-56399-172-1

Have You Made the Wonderful Discovery of the Spirit-filled Life?

In this timeless tract used for decades, you will discover how to live in moment-by-moment dependence on God. ISBN 1-56399-020-2

GOD: Discover His Character

In this thorough, easy-to-grasp book, Dr. Bright helps make God knowable as few books (save the Bible itself) have done. Based on more than five decades of intense, personal study, Dr. Bright's penetrating insights into God's character—and its significance to mankind—are certain to energize your walk with God. ISBN 1-56399-125-X

For a complete list of the Discover God family of products, including a 13-lesson video curriculum, visit our website at www.nlpdirect.com.

Living Supernaturally in Christ

A refreshing cascade of hope, power and renewal, *Living Supernaturally in Christ* vividly illustrates the many benefits of knowing Jesus Christ personally. With rare clarity, it reveals how your relationship with Christ will help you live in harmony with God's plan. It will in - troduce you to scriptural passages and principles that convey the incomparable blessing we share in Christ, and help you open the door to victorious Christian living. ISBN 1-56399-146-2

The Supernatural You

Written in a convenient, take-along format, this booklet helps you discover and live according to your new, supernatural identity in Christ. The booklet outlines five essential steps to living supernaturally in Christ, made easily memorable by the acrostic CROSS. As you apply these biblical truths, you'll discover a life of incomparable power, liberating freedom, triumph over adversity, everlasting peace, and infinite joy. *The Supernatural You* is an ideal companion booklet to *Living Supernaturally in Christ* and *Why Do Christians Suffer?* ISBN 1-56399-147-0

Why Do Christians Suffer?

Why do Christians suffer? It's a valid question that many believers—even some nonbelievers—wrestle with from time to time. As a stand-alone booklet or a companion piece to Dr. Bright's book *Living Supernaturally in Christ*, this informative purse or pocket guide will direct you to the Bible's illuminating answers. By remembering the acrostic TRIUMPH, you can experience God's peace even in the midst of adversity, pain, and heartache. Ideal for personal reference or to share with friends in need. ISBN 1-56399-149-7

Children's Discipleship Series

Based on the best-selling *Ten Basic Steps Toward Christian Maturity*, the foundational discipleship material used by Campus Crusade for Christ for more than four decades. Use each book as a quarterly topical study or the series as a 52-lesson discipleship curriculum. Lessons contain guided discussion and questions, games for verse memorization, reproducible sheets for in-class or follow-up activities, application activities, and weekly assignment to build discipleship principles into students' lives. No student workbook needed!

Book 1: Beginning the Christian Adventure

Introduces children to the thrill of walking with Jesus day by day.

Includes lessons on how Jesus can help them overcome problems and how they can study the Bible, pray effectively, and win spiritual battles through God's Spirit. ISBN 1-56399-151-9

Book 2: Discovering Our Awesome God
Introduces students to the wonders and awesome nature of God-the Father, the Son, and the Holy Spirit—and how to talk to our loving God. ISBN 1-56399-152-7

Book 3: Growing in God's Word
Gives students a foundation in how the Bible is arranged and how the Old and New Testament are God's plan for humanity. Also includes practical applications for using God's Word daily.
ISBN 1-56399-153-5

Book 4: Building an Active Faith
Shows students how to build their faith through obeying God, giving back part of what they have to Him, and sharing their faith with others. ISBN 1-56399-154-3

Other Books by Bill Bright
Beyond All Limits (*co-author*)
Blessed Child (*co-author*)
Building a Home in a Pull-Apart World
Come Help Change the World
The Coming Revival (*1996 Gold Medallion Finalist*)
The Greatest Lesson I've Ever Learned (*Series Editor*)
Holy Spirit: Key to Supernatural Living
Life Without Equal
Man Without Equal
Promises: A Daily Guide for Supernatural Living
Quiet Moments with Bill Bright
Red Sky in the Morning (*co-author*)
The Secret
The Transforming Power of Fasting & Prayer
Witnessing Without Fear (*1988 Gold Medallion Award Winner*)

Biography

William R. Bright

Founder, Chairman, and President Emeritus,
Campus Crusade for Christ International

From a small beginning in 1951, the organization he began now has a presence in 196 countries in areas representing 99.6% of the world's population. Campus Crusade for Christ has more than 70 ministries and major projects, utilizing more than 25,000 full-time and 500,000 trained volunteer staff. Each ministry is designed to help fulfill the Great Commission, Christ's command to help carry the gospel of God's love and forgiveness in Christ to every person on earth.

Born in Coweta, Oklahoma, on October 19, 1921, Bright graduated with honors from Northeastern State University, and completed five years of graduate study at Princeton and Fuller Theological Seminaries. He holds five honorary doctorate degrees from prestigious institutions and has received numerous other recognitions, including the ECPA Gold Medallion Lifetime Achievement Award (2001), the Golden Angel Award as International Churchman of the Year (1982), and the $1.1 million Templeton Prize for Progress in Religion (1996), which he dedicated to promoting fasting and prayer throughout the world. He has received the first-ever Lifetime Achievement Award from his alma mater (2001).

Bright has authored more than 100 books, booklets, videos and audio tapes, as well as thousands of articles and pamphlets, some of which have been printed in most major languages and distributed by the millions. Among his books are: *Come Help Change the World*, *The Secret*, *The Holy Spirit*, *A Man Without Equal*, *A Life Without Equal*, *The Coming Revival*, *The Transforming Power of Fasting & Prayer*, *Red Sky in the Morning* (co-author), *GOD: Discover His Character*, *Living Super-naturally in Christ*, and the booklet *Have You Heard of the Four Spiritual*

Laws? (which has an estimated 2.5 billion circulation). He has also been responsible for many individual initiatives in ministry, particularly in evangelism. For example, the *JESUS* film, which he conceived and financed through Campus Crusade, has, by latest estimates, been viewed by over 4.6 billion people in 236 nations and provinces.

Bright and his wife, Vonette, who assisted him in founding Campus Crusade for Christ, live in Orlando, Florida. Their two sons, Zac and Brad, and their wives, Terry and Katherine, are also in full-time Christian ministry.